ILLUSTRATED
GUIDE TO
SHAKER FURNITURE

ROBERT F. W. MEADER

Director of the
SHAKER MUSEUM
Old Chatham, N.Y.

DOVER PUBLICATIONS, INC., NEW YORK

Published in Canada by General Publishing Company, Ltd., 30 Lesmill Road, Don Mills, Toronto, Ontario.
Published in the United Kingdom by Constable and Company, Ltd., 10 Orange Street, London WC 2.

Illustrated Guide to Shaker Furniture is a new work, first published by Dover Publications, Inc., in 1972.

International Standard Book Number: 0-486-22819-3
Library of Congress Catalog Card Number: 74-164732

Manufactured in the United States of America
Dover Publications, Inc.
180 Varick Street
New York, N. Y. 10014

FOREWORD

It is a particularly real pleasure for me as founder of the Shaker Museum to write a foreword for Robert Meader's new book. I first became associated with Robert in 1958 when I asked him to come to the Museum as Director. During the subsequent years he has done an extremely fine job and I must say that I believe our joint efforts have added a great deal to the institution. Sometimes I think we are better known internationally than locally.

Robert Meader's knowledge and appreciation of the Shakers and their works have increased constantly until now he certainly must be accepted as one of the foremost experts on this extraordinary phase in our American history. This, his new book, may well be read by everybody, from the expert to the beginner who wishes to find out some of the more intriguing details about Shaker workmanship and furniture design. I therefore thoroughly recommend this book to a wide range of readers.

John S. Williams
Founder and Chairman of the Board
Shaker Museum,
Old Chatham, N. Y.

INTRODUCTION

The Shakers, who are the oldest communal organization in the United States, originated in England with a small group of dissident Quakers near Manchester, whose beliefs were influenced by the doctrines and practices of the "French Prophets," Protestants exiled from that kingdom in 1689, some of whom came to England.

The leader of the little group was Mother Ann Lee (or Lees) (1736–1784), daughter of a Manchester blacksmith, who married one of her father's young apprentices, by whom she had four children, all of whom died in early infancy, a tragedy which probably influenced Mother Ann to insist on the rule of celibacy for her followers.

In 1774, following a stormy period in England, she and eight disciples took ship for America, landing in New York City. There her husband soon deserted her, and after two years of urban hardship the little group moved upriver to Albany, on the outskirts of which one of them had secured land in the Manor of Rensselaerwyck; the site is today the Albany County Airport. In this sequestered spot they lived quietly supporting themselves by jobs in the area and by farming. A few converts were made of the neighbors, but the time was not yet ripe for the extension of the new gospel.

That time came in 1781. Accompanied by a few of the faithful, Mother Ann undertook a two-year missionary journey that covered Massachusetts, upper Connecticut, western Rhode Island and a few of the border townships of New York, particularly New Lebanon. Converts came flocking by scores, and unfortunately so did conflicts with the law. Worn out by her exertions, Mother Ann returned to Niskeyuna (later Watervliet) in 1784, where she died that fall, having first made provision for a successor, Father James Whittaker, a young English convert.

In 1787 the first commune was organized "in Gospel Order" at New Lebanon, followed later that year by the organizing of Mother Ann's own little settlement. Within the next seven years the nine New England communes came into being, then, in the first two decades of the next century, the four Ohio and two Kentucky communities were organized, sparked by the famous Kentucky Revival of 1800.

There were, altogether, eighteen of these Shaker enclaves, with an estimated population of some 6000 Believers at their height around 1850. At the present writing there are two still in existence, numbering but fifteen Sisters.

The outstanding tenets of the Shaker faith were belief in the dual nature of Deity (Father and Mother God) and of the Savior (Jesus and Mother Ann); celibacy; community of goods; parity of the sexes in both administration and responsibility; pacifism; temperance in all things; universal brotherhood; confession of sins, and growth of the inner life through regeneration, prayer and purity of living.

During their heyday the Believers' agricultural prosperity was increased by a multiplicity of industries which made them wealthy, such as the herbal medicine and seed businesses, the manufacture of chairs (the only furniture made for public sale), the production of brooms and many other enterprises. Changing times, however, and the rise of commercial industry made their products obsolete; prospects of high wages rendered the communal, monastic life unattractive to outsiders, and converts failed to keep up membership. Today the Shakers are remembered chiefly for the superb furniture which graced the many buildings and shops of their once-prosperous and populous villages, now largely vanished.

This book is not intended as a treatise on Shaker furniture history or styles; the subject has been adequately dealt with in other volumes. Rather, it is written for collectors and antique dealers who wish to be able to identify more accurately pieces which they possess or which they hope to acquire. As interest in the Shakers and their crafts has increased in late years, so has the tendency on the part of enthusiasts hopefully to ascribe to Shaker provenance pieces which never were nor ever could have been made by them.

While every effort has been made to be accurate and authoritative, and while every piece pictured and described has been authenticated, one must not assume that the points illustrated are the only ones to be found on genuine Shaker pieces. It must be realized that the Believers, like craftsmen everywhere, grew weary of sameness, and consequently showed infinite variety within the general Shaker context. One cannot too much emphasize that it is very often not an *individual* feature that will identify a piece as Shaker, but rather the *totality* of features. In short, after dealing with these pieces enough one will come to realize that the article under consideration "feels" right or does not. This book, then, is written to help give foundation for such a feeling.

The beginning collector (and occasionally even the advanced one), as well as the antique dealer having access to supposed pieces, naturally seeks certainty of identification. Unhappily, this too often cannot be supplied. However, enough details can be given to make attribution reasonably sure, and thus to prevent the collector or dealer from going too far astray. Any advanced collector in any field shortly realizes that the more he knows the less he knows, and often the less sure he is of attribution.

This book does not claim omniscience nor ultimate authority. The author has been closely associated with Shaker artifacts for ten years, and during that time, in addition to his own researches and discoveries, has had the inestimable privilege of association with a number of individuals who have been intimately concerned with collecting and identifying Shaker furniture for a far longer period. Among these are Mr. John S. Williams, Sr., founder and Chairman of the Board of the Shaker Museum at Old Chatham, N. Y.; Dr. Charles W. Upton of Troy, Vice-President of the same Museum, and owner of one of the outstanding private collections of Shakeriana in the country; the late Dr. Edward D. Andrews of Pittsfield, Mass., and Mrs. Andrews; and Dr. Gerald J. J. McCue of the Massachusetts Institute of Technology. Of all of these, Dr. and Mrs. Andrews have probably studied the subject in greatest depth and written with most authority. Their *Shaker Furniture* (1937; Dover reprint) and *Religion in Wood* (1966) are still considered classics in the field.

The author extends his gratitude and thanks to the following institutions and individuals for their courteous permission to photograph pieces of furniture in their possession: the Shaker Museum, Old Chatham, N. Y.; the Hancock Shaker Community, Inc., Pittsfield, Mass.; the Western Reserve Historical Society, Cleveland, Ohio; the Warren County Historical Society, Lebanon, Ohio; Shakertown at Pleasant Hill, Inc., Harrodsburg, Ky.; the Kentucky Museum, Western Kentucky University, Bowling Green, Ky.; St. Mark's Monastery, South Union, Ky.; Shakertown at South Union, Ky.; the Shaker Museum, Sabbathday Lake Shakers, Poland Spring, Me.; Dr. and Mrs. Charles W. Upton, Troy, N. Y.; Mr. Sylvester Labanowski, Troy, N. Y.; Mrs. William Kline, Lebanon Springs, N. Y.; Prof. Gustave Nelson, Troy, N. Y.; Mr. and Mrs. Edgar Clerk, Malden Bridge, N. Y., and Mr. Karl Mendel, Southampton, N. Y.

All photographs, except where otherwise credited, were taken by the author.

Robert F. W. Meader

Old Chatham, N. Y.

LOCATION OF
The
SHAKER COMMUNITIES

LEGEND

✹ EXTANT VILLAGES
● DEFUNCT VILLAGES
◑ SHORT-LIVED VILLAGES

1 Alfred (1793–1931)
2 Canterbury (1792–present)
3 Enfield, Conn. (1792–1917)
4 Enfield, N.H. (1793–1918)
5 Groveland (1836–1892)
6 Hancock (1790–1960)
7 Harvard (1791–1919)
8 Mt. Lebanon (1787–1947)
9 North Union (1826–1889)
10 Pleasant Hill (1814–1910)
11 Sabbathday Lake (1794–present)
12 Shirley (1793–1909)
13 South Union (1811–1922)
14 Tyringham (1792–1875)
15 Union Village (1812–1910)
16 Watervliet, N.Y. (1787–1938)
17 Watervliet, Ohio (1813–1900)
18 West Union (1810–1827)
19 Whitewater (1824–1907)

A Gorham (1808–1819)
B Sodus Bay (1826–1836; moved to Groveland)
C White Oak (1898–1902)
D Narcoossee (1896–c. 1913)

CONTENTS

1. CHAIRS AND FOOTSTOOLS

Shaker craftsmanship in furniture, like other aspects of their life and activities, displays an honesty and integrity of design and construction. Brother Thomas Whitaker, O.S.B., of St. Mark's Monastery, South Union, Ky., in an unpublished manuscript entitled *A Benedictine-Shaker Link* (1968), has some very pertinent comments on this subject:

> Most people viewing Shaker handicraft see the simple lines and the beauty inherent in the product. They fail to realize the religious motivation behind the Shaker craftsman and his work. Mother Ann had given her followers an injunction: "Hands to work and hearts to God." Thus, the Shaker craftsman approached his work with honesty before God, desiring to use his God-given talents to work the material which had likewise come from God. There was, therefore, a union of forces in creativity between the craftsman and God wherein a sense of cooperation and truthfulness prevailed in fashioning the finished product. It was this factor, rather than a conscious striving for the aesthetic, that resulted in the attractive charm of Shaker products. Another saying of Mother Ann was: "Build as though you were to live for a thousand years, and as you would do if you knew you were to die tomorrow." This accounts for the sturdy Shaker buildings, manifesting a simple dignity without need of elaborate ornamentation. Their furniture and handicraft items are characterized by simple lines, utility and durability. The Shaker craftsmen achieved beauty through a sense of balance, conciseness, strength (though of delicate appearance), and an enduring simplicity. Their products were the forerunners of our present day functional furniture.

Long before Louis Sullivan had popularized the slogan "Form follows function," the Shakers had been practicing it. Mother Ann was always inveighing against dirt—and, by extension, elaborations in furniture were dirt-catchers. Further, the Millennial Laws of the Church spoke out strongly for simplicity of form and the avoidance of elaboration for its own sake or for that of the beauty which catches, gulls and distracts the eye from the heaven-ward path. True, in the 1880's and 1890's the craftsmen, while adhering to their traditional integrity of workmanship, occasionally forgot the functionalism of earlier days and the dicta of the Millennial Laws, and fell into the trap of worldly, Victorian elaboration. Even then, however, their Shaker heritage usually restrained them from the most violent of excesses in design.

Believers did not, for the most part at least, originate any furniture forms, contrary to the opinion held by many. One should never forget that before a person became a Shaker, he was of the "World." This means that householders lived with and often made furniture which in design and construction was identical with similar pieces in common use in the areas where they resided. For instance, trestle tables have been, in form and design, used for millennia; those common to New England and the South stem directly from English medieval and Renaissance prototypes. Why, then, should a cabinetmaker who had left the World to become a Believer fail to bring with him the ideas of design and construction which he had been using all his life? A dining table, say, would be needed and he would be asked to make one; why not make one after the pattern which he knew—simplified, of course, to accord with Shaker principles of functionalism?

To these considerations should be added another, alluded to in the quotation above from Bro. Thomas Whitaker—the religio-social background. We must never forget that the Shakers were in reality a Protestant monastic order, and the religious motivation was never far removed from their daily lives. This is brought out very well in Alan Gowans's essay "Spiritual Functionalism in Shaker Furniture," found on pp. 15–20 of Andrews's well-known *Religion in Wood*. Mr. Gowans brings out the point that the Northeastern Shakers were inheritors of the Calvinistic, stern and repressive way of life, and that the furniture made by the New Yorkers and New Englanders reflected this starkness. The Shakers, being members of a strict religious order, refined this style to its quintessence. This makes a great deal of sense. Why, then, did Western Shaker furniture display so much more variety, especially in Kentucky, and so much greater richness of detail? The answer is probably to be found in the migration patterns of settlers along the southern tier of states. Kentucky was settled in many instances by Virginians, many of them on their way to Arkansas and the Far West. Virginia had been settled by Anglicans, whose Church was officially established in that province. Anglicanism is notably more relaxed than Calvinism, and was not observably put off by beauty for its own sake. As for Ohio, although many of the settlers there were from New England and New York, the sternness of Yankee Calvinism had probably been muted somewhat by the influence from Kentucky and neighboring states with a different ethos. This resulted in more variety of form and detail than found in the East, but less than found in Kentucky.

When workmen brought up in and surrounded by local cabinetmaking traditions became Believers, it was inevitable that they should continue to work within the framework of this training, which was reinforced and extended by the almost fanatical teaching of Mother Ann against all superfluity. But even her strictures could only modify the elegance of Southern furniture details, very probably in part because of the geographical separation and distance from the Shaker North. The Kentucky colonies and some of those in Ohio always posed administrative and doctrinal problems to the Parent Ministry in New Lebanon; furniture styles would naturally follow the same independent line.

Even in Kentucky and Ohio, however, the traditional Shaker restraint is always present except at the very end of furniture production, when both North and West tended to fall into the Victorian trap. But even the worst excesses of Victorianism were avoided save in rare and isolated pieces, so strong were Shaker traditions.

However, even within a given community basic designs were often mutated and adapted to particular uses. This is characteristic of functionalism as a whole, and is especially true of the Shakers, who had to adapt furniture not only to a particular spot, but to a particular function dictated by the needs of a religious community. Take, for example, the common candlestand, used in most Colonial homes to hold the chambersticks which one picked up to light one's way to bed. The Shakers also had candlestands; by enlarging the top and hanging runthrough drawers beneath it, they constructed an exceedingly attractive and practical sewing stand. Then, as the burden of sewing and dressmaking increased with the growing number of adherents to the sect, small chests of drawers were devised—*this* seems to have been an original form!—to hold sewing materials and implements. If a pull-out slide was provided to increase the working surface, they were called sewing desks.

To collectors of furniture, the Believers are probably best known for their chairs; indeed, a rocker was used as part of the design for the gold transfer which the Mt. Lebanon* factories put on their products. Very few case pieces or other furniture types were manufactured for sale to the World and such pieces, almost without exception, were obtained from dying communities and finally found their way into private hands. The antique dealers in earliest days often bought such pieces directly from the Shakers; nowadays these generally come from private owners who so obtained them. With chairs, however, there was a different story. Of all the different types of furniture, it is probable that the chair is the most essential form. One can eat standing, or off one's lap; one can sleep on the floor; but it is difficult to *sit* or do anything else on the floor for any length of time. Therefore chairs are vital to home furnishing. Furthermore, chairmaking is a highly specialized form of cabinetry, a fact which is attested to by the number of companies devoted to making nothing else. To manufacture chairs individually is both time-consuming and unsatisfactory: to be efficient, one has to devise and set up jigs to bore stretcher holes to given depths and at proper intervals and angles. These considerations do not obtain for the most part with tables, desks, cupboards, etc. Also, chairs are not bulky to store and to stockpile, and they are reasonably easy to buy and to transport. It is therefore most understandable that the Believers concentrated on chairs as a marketable form of cabinetry.

---

*Prior to 1861 this original community was known as New Lebanon; after the establishment of a sub-postoffice in that year, to distinguish the new office from the old, the Shakers and the Government adopted the name Mt. Lebanon, by which name it is generally still known. Where one can date furniture in general, this distinction is used in this book.

Another fact motivated the Shakers in not producing larger pieces for general sale: the amount of lumber needing to be stockpiled. A blanket chest, dining table or other large piece requires a very considerable amount of lumber; a chair, relatively little. And, even for the efficient and well-organized Shakers, time was a consideration; to make a chair by assembly-line techniques consumed vastly less time than the making of a case piece with its planing, dovetailing, paneling, breadboarding, fitting and assembling. A higher percentage of profit could be realized with a much smaller expenditure of time per piece.

These factors all seemed to weigh heavily with Bro. Robert M. Wagan (1833–1883) of Mt. Lebanon's Second, later South, Family. From earliest days most, if not all, the communities made chairs for sale to the public over and above those needed for domestic use; this production was, at best, haphazard and sporadic, and was small in numbers of units produced. Brother Robert, in 1863, came to the conclusion that by properly setting up his shop he could produce chairs in quantity; with due attention to sales outlets, advertising, production costs and pricing, he could return to the communal treasury a very handsome profit.

And so it proved to be. In 1873 the business was thoroughly reorganized, new factories were built at the adjoining South Family, and the latest and best machinery was installed. Production really began in earnest. Brother Robert (by then he was Elder Robert of the South Family) set up his enterprise under the name of "R. M. Wagan & Co."; the "& Co." consisted of those brethren and sisters assigned to work under his direction. Until production finally ceased around 1935, long after Brother Robert had died, this corporate name continued in use, a custom common to all Shaker industries. Thus continuity of name and product was assured.

The earliest manufacture of chairs prior to 1850 seems to have produced the ladder-back straight or side chairs for the most part, although rockers had been known and made from nearly the beginning; after Brother Robert's reorganizing of the industry at Mt. Lebanon, the vast proportion of chairs seem to have been rockers. This was probably due to the greater comfort of such a type, and also undoubtedly reflected popular taste at the time—a sensitivity which marked most Shaker industrialists.

Wagan's chair catalogues* listed eight basic, numbered models, ranging from No. 0, the smallest child's chair, to No. 7, the largest adult chair. With the several variations of each type, there were in all 46 different models, usually with a choice of seating. If to these 46 "canonical" models we add the uncatalogued spindle-backs and bentwoods, we arrive at the astonishing sum of 52 models (each of the spindle-backs is found in at least two sizes, and the bentwoods in four). And occasional rare "sports" are found, like the high chairs and double armchairs.

Aside from direct factory sales, outlets (frequently multiple) were provided in many cities, such as Boston, New York, Pittsfield, Chicago and many others; in 1888, indeed, efforts were made to establish sales outlets in England

---

*One of these catalogues is reproduced in its entirety in the Appendix to the present book.

and France, but nothing seems to have come of this ambitious scheme. And since Mt. Lebanon produced by far the most chairs for sale, and sold them most widely, people of today naturally tend to think of chairs when they think of Shakers.

No statistics are available on the total production put out by the Second and South Families over the years, but the number certainly reached into the tens of thousands of units. At the Philadelphia Centennial Exposition of 1876, the Shakers had a display booth exhibiting chairs and footstools, and sales boomed thereafter.

Throughout their history the Shakers used all four of the usual forms of seating: cane, rush, wood splint and fabric tape. The overwhelming favorite seems to have been tape (or "listing," as the Believers called it), which seems to have been used originally in England, though this has not been, and possibly cannot be, documented. At first, and for many years, the tape was handwoven in home-grown wool; afterward commercially woven woolen worsted was used (probably around 1850, though the date is not certain) and later cotton canvas. The latter is still obtainable, though in coarser form; it has, however, the unfortunate habit of fading badly, especially the red. Earlier machine tapes were much less susceptible to this change; the Shakers bought them in white only, and dyed them to the colors they wanted. Both the early commercial tapes and the original handwoven ones were colored with vegetable dyes, and were notably fade-resistant.

There were probably several reasons, mostly practical, for the popularity of the fabric tape. It was relatively inexpensive to make; it wore well, probably better than most of the other materials; it did not pinch or snag clothing; it was more comfortable; and lastly, it gave a chance to introduce some color, which added to the pleasantness and charm of rooms. A cushion was first made, with wide extended flaps on all four sides; this was stuffed with almost anything available—straw, clean old cloth, curled hair, shavings, even sawdust. Inserted inside the middle of the four top or seat rounds, the flaps of the cushion were wrapped around these rounds and secured; the weight of the body was basically supported by the cushion. The tape was then woven over the cushion top and bottom, thereby giving protection against wear and adding to the support. Some varieties of the late Mt. Lebanon chairs were upholstered in a sort of coarse plush called "shag" by the Shakers and made, like velvet, over wires which were later withdrawn; the top of the resulting loops was then cut or sheared off.

A variety of chairs fairly common to the Wagan line, and apparently peculiar to Shaker manufacture, was equipped not with finials, but with a curved dowel bar attached to the top of the back posts. Frequently called by antique dealers and others a "shawl rail," it should properly be spoken of as a "cushion rail." To this was attached by narrow tape loops a back cushion of the "shag" mentioned above, usually with a border of some color contrasting with that of the main body of the chair. Shawls may indeed have been draped over this bar, but the primary intent was to provide a means for attaching the cushion.

One of the minor refinements attributable apparently to the Shakers alone was the tilter. Evidently the brethren could not be trained not to lean back in their ladder-back chairs, so some brother in the first quarter of the last century conceived the idea of the tilter. This was basically a ball-and-socket foot inserted into the back legs of ladder-backs produced in the Northeast. The swiveling foot was held in place by a rawhide thong drawn out through the side of the leg and pegged in place When the sitter leaned back, the foot stayed flat on the floor, thus sparing rugs and flooring. Since the wooden cup-shaped sockets were prone to split out with the pressure, in 1852 a patent was taken out for a tilter in metal, called the "boot." Essentially this was the same thing, except that the socket, of pewter, fitted like a ferule over the end of the leg; the ball foot was held in place in the same way. Another version had the foot held in by a bezel rim. Apparently very few were made; only two or three are known, so the experiment (for such it seems to have been) was not considered successful. Oddly enough a few of the low-backed dining chairs were so equipped. This seems peculiar, since after-meal lounging was not permitted, and thus there would have been little or no incentive for tilting back in them; furthermore, the low back gave very little body leverage for such a maneuver.

In addition to those chairs manufactured for the carriage trade and illustrated in the catalogues, there were many other types made exclusively for domestic use. Perhaps the commonest of these were the dining chairs, made with a low back of one or two slats. This was to facilitate pushing the chairs under the unskirted top of the dining table, and thus allow easier setting and clearing thereof. Inasmuch as meals were eaten largely in silence, and at the end the community rose and went back to work, there was neither time nor incentive for relaxing at the table as we do today; higher-backed and more comfortable chairs were thus not needed. Some models of dining chairs used in Ohio and Kentucky had spindle backs topped with a broad thick slat; this was uncommon in the North.

Derived in form from the dining chairs were the loom and ironing chairs. These had the same low back but taller legs. In addition, loom chairs usually had seats that sloped somewhat forward to give freer play to legs in working the loom pedals.

Another type was the so-called "revolver," said by the Shakers to have originated at Enfield, N. H., though made elsewhere as well. This was a swivel chair rather like a piano stool, except that the height was generally not adjustable. The back was of the comb variety with a curved dowel top; the spindles were originally of wood, and later of heavy iron wire rods. They are said to have been designed originally for use in the schoolrooms.

Analogous to and frequently derived from the chair was the bench, appearing in a number of different forms, none commercially produced for sale. The simplest was the meetinghouse bench, used also in early days in the dining rooms. This bench was very simple, with plank top and ends, the latter diagonally braced to the top. The plank ends were generally provided with triangular or semicircular cut at the bottom. A more elaborate form was the comb-backed "deacon's" bench, with a slab seat and with but four turned legs (six, in very long ones). These legs had front-to-back stretchers only, with surprisingly no longitudinal ones. They were thus subject to more wracking than they should have been. It is odd that the furniture makers, excellent craftsmen as they were, should have even considered so unstable a design. The comb-back probably derived ultimately from the Windsor chair.

An odd form of bench made in the late nineteenth century was the double armchair, apparently restricted to Mt. Lebanon, and appearing extremely rarely. Only two are known to the writer. They looked like a very wide, standard No. 7 armchair with a double back, and seated two people. They had taped seats and slat backs.

A persistent legend has it that if a Mt. Lebanon "production" chair did not have a number stamped on it or a decal, it was intended only for home consumption and not for sale. This is spectacularly refuted by the so-called chapel chairs, made for and used only in the Mt. Lebanon meetinghouse, and never sold commercially First introduced in August of 1887, all bore the model number 3. These particular chairs were built for and equipped with punched-plywood seats obtained from some commercial manufacturer, quite possibly Gardner & Company of New York, who had a large bent-plywood furniture booth at the Centennial Exposition of 1876, where the Shakers also exhibited.

A few chairs turn up from time to time with removable slip seats, which were upholstered in some sort of sculptured plush, or the Shaker-made "shag." These were generally of the large-armed type. The seat was supported on seat stretchers across the front and back, but not along the sides; the plank over which the upholstery was applied was cut out at the corners to fit around the posts.

Chairs made both for sale and for home use in Ohio and Kentucky exhibit many more variations in arms, runners and finials than their Northern prototypes; this is especially true in Kentucky. They are very apt also to be heavier and more coarsely built; some are actually clumsy, at least by Northern Shaker standards. In Ohio, and to a somewhat less degree in Kentucky, straight chairs and armchairs generally have legs terminating in a decidedly sharp taper, a form seen in non-Shaker chairs from Ohio to Texas. Ladderbacks usually have four rather than the Northern three slats, which generally are corner-notched on the upper sides; each of these slats very often has fine nails or wooden pegs in each end, in contradistinction to Northern custom, which fixed only the top slat, and that with a single peg at each end.

2

1

5

1. Early side chair from Harvard, Mass. It is unusual in that it has four slats, a characteristic of Western Shaker, especially Ohio; those slats, however, have an entirely different shape. The legs on this chair have been cut down. (Private collection)

2. Detail of the finial of the chair in Fig. 1. The shape of this is very different from most Shaker finials.

3. Early Mt. Lebanon (N. Y.) side chair, with tilters on the back legs; plain finish. The seat tape is probably a later Shaker replacement of an original handwoven one. Probably c. 1840. Seat is 16" high. (Shaker Museum, Old Chatham, N. Y.)

4. Side view of the chair in Fig. 3. Note the slanted posts. This is a stage midway between the earliest form with straight, vertical posts, and the late form with vertical legs but with the back posts bent. The slanted posts seen here made a more comfortable piece of furniture. Note that the thin walls of the socket holding the tilters have split out with tipping back, and have had to be reinforced (by the Shakers) with tin collars.

5. Detail of the chair in Figs. 3 and 4. The top slat only is pegged. The finial has a rather sharp cut-in below the head, with a slight shoulder or ridge between the head and the shoulder at the top of the post. This last feature is much more pronounced on the early Watervliet chairs.

3

4

6

6. Side chair, Mt. Lebanon, c. 1852. Curly maple frame, cane seat. The chair is equipped with the "boot," a patented tilter made of pewter. The idea was patented (#8871) by George O. Donnell, an associate of Elder Robert M. Wagan, on March 2, 1852, in a slightly different form. Only three chairs thus equipped are currently known; this one may very well be a pilot model. (Shaker Museum, Old Chatham, N. Y.)

7. Caning on the chair in Fig. 6. Note edge-binding to conceal the holes in the side rails through which the canes passed.

8. Underside of the chair in Fig. 6, showing method of caning and the form of rounds employed for this purpose.

9. Patented "boot" or metal tilter of the chair in Fig. 6. For some reason, this idea was given up almost immediately. Of the three known "boots," only this one has both ferule and ball-foot made of pewter; the other two have a pewter ferule and brass foot, conforming more closely to the Donnell patent, in which the foot was clinched in by the rim of the socket. On this particular chair, the foot was held in as were the wooden prototypes, by a rawhide thong passed through the post from the bottom of the socket, and pegged. The "boot" was evidently invented to do away with the tendency of the wooden sockets to split out in use. (Photo by Lees Studio, Chatham, N. Y.)

10. Detail of the leg of the chair in Fig. 6, showing the scribe mark used as a guide for positioning holes for the stretchers and slats. Many consider these marks to be proof of the authenticity of Shaker pieces; however, most chairmakers from earliest times, both Shaker and non-Shaker, used them. Of themselves they prove nothing.

7

8

9

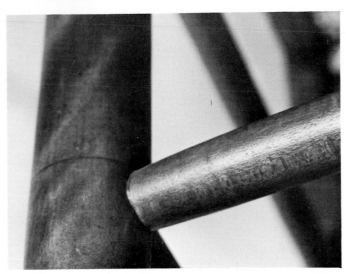

10

11. Enfield, N. H., side chair, equipped with tilters on the back legs. Chairs from this community were characterized by extreme attenuation (weight, about 5½ lbs.) and candle-flame finials, generally with a delicate single or double scribe mark around the thickest part of the finials. (Shaker Museum, Old Chatham, N. Y.)

12. Candle-flame finial of the chair shown in Fig. 11. While the scribe marks on the posts were guides for mortising and drilling, those on the finials were simple decoration. The slats were beveled on the top edge *after* insertion into the post, as it would have been extremely difficult to make a bevel-slanted mortise.

13. Tilter of the chair in Fig. 11. Notice the method by which the ball-foot was held into the socket. This particular tilter has been replaced; the hardened rawhide had to be drilled out, and the new thong was then tacked in place instead of being pegged, as originally.

14. Mt. Lebanon No. 2 straight chair, 1890–1920 period. Last stage of back-post design, in which the posts were bent to give greater comfort. For the bending device, see Fig. 83. (Shaker Museum, Old Chatham, N. Y.)

15. Variants on the side chair. These are dining chairs from Watervliet, N. Y. Northern dining chairs were of this type, with either one or two slats; those in the West more usually had slab seats, and the backs were spindle-supported slat-topped: like Northern chairs of this sort, they were low-backed to allow the chair to be slid beneath the table top. Canterbury had the odd habit of equipping some dining chairs with tilters. In the illustration, the chair at the left is the earlier, and is without finials; the one at the right is later and is more sophisticated. It has nipple finials and a turned front round, a decidedly late and atypical feature. Splint seats, 15½″ high. (Shaker Museum, Old Chatham, N. Y.)

16. Detail of the chair shown at the right in Fig. 15. Note the nipple finial, apparently restricted largely if not entirely to the Watervliet community. Note also the heavy bevel on the top of the slat, another feature found largely at Watervliet.

11

12

13

15

14

16

17

18

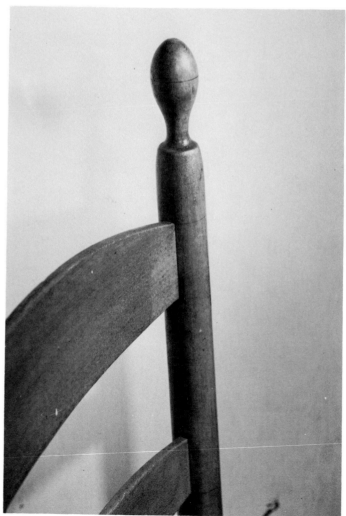

19

17. Three low-backed chairs, based on the dining chair. The one in the center is an ironing chair from Canterbury, N. H. The other two chairs, from Mt. Lebanon, are possibly dining chairs, but were more probably made for sale as boudoir chairs to the carriage trade. They were products of the South Family and were designed by William Perkins. (Shaker Museum, Old Chatham, N. Y.; photo by Lees Studio, Chatham, N. Y.)

18. Rocking chairs probably developed from cradles, and at first were made by affixing runners to side chairs, as here. This chair, from Canterbury, was originally designed as a tilter, but the tilts were apparently never inserted. Since the legs were not cut down to accommodate the thickness of these early "suicide" runners, the chair is uncomfortably high, and most unstable. The seat is of very old handwoven tape in blue-gray and red. (Shaker Museum, Old Chatham, N. Y.)

19. Finial of the chair in Fig. 18, of the inverted bowling pin type, with a scribe mark around by the entasis, reminiscent of Enfield, N. H. The top slat is, interestingly, not pegged, but made fast with a small copper nail.

20. Mt. Lebanon rocker, late South Family type. These chairs were given a high varnish finish over a mahogany stain, and were notable for being high in the seat, which is 19¼" from the floor. They were also four-slat, as contrasted with the usual Mt. Lebanon chair of three slats. (Shaker Museum, Old Chatham, N. Y.)

21. Finial of the rocker in Fig. 20, also a design by William Perkins. This is a decadent variant of the early type; the shoulder has here been exaggerated into a ring or collar. While it is rare to find an identifying mark or decal on these variants, one three-slat chair has been found with a wrap-around decal and a No. 6 stamped on the back of the top slat. Four-slat armchairs had a post too long for Shaker lathe-beds; the finial was separately turned and doweled to the post.

22. Sewing chair, Mt. Lebanon. This was essentially a No. 4 standard chair, with taped back and cushion rail, equipped with two under-seat drawers, end-stopped to prevent their being pulled all the way out and dumped. These chairs were made in limited quantities, probably on special order; few are known. (Shaker Museum, Old Chatham, N. Y.; photo by Lees Studio, Chatham, N. Y.)

21

20

22

23

25

24

23. Detail of the earliest type of armed rocker. The mushroom is turned on the top of the post, which the arm clasps, and into which it is doweled. Construction is very heavy and very early. Probably New Lebanon. (Shaker Museum, Old Chatham, N. Y.)

24. Next earliest type of armed rocker. Canterbury. Maple frame, pegged joints, "suicide runners" and vertically scrolled arms. (Shaker Museum, Old Chatham, N. Y.)

25. Detail of the rocker in Fig. 24. Probably the ancestry of this form, well known in early America, was Jacobean. Pegged into the delicately turned post, the arm is peculiarly graceful.

26. Tablet-arm chair from Watervliet. The four slats are heavily beveled on the top edge, and the back posts terminate in nipple finials. The pegged scroll-arm is characteristic of chairs made around 1825. It is highly probable that the runners are considerably later and were put on to convert an armchair to a rocker. The posts now terminate not in a peg, as they would if the runners were original, but in a rectangular tenon, pegged into a mortise in the runner. Dark green painted finish, splint bottom. (Shaker Museum, Old Chatham, N. Y.)

27. Detail of the tablet of the chair illustrated in Fig. 26, showing the method of affixing the tablet to the post, which is turned and designed to receive it. Note the characteristic chamfering of the brace, which is pegged to the button termination of the post.

26

27

28

29

28. Wheelchair from Watervliet, made from a very early rocker. Maple, natural finish, splint seat. The wheels are made on the general pattern of a spinning wheel; the one-piece, wrap-around felloe is grooved to receive a rope tire, which must have been spliced together, and is long gone. The back is made adjustable by a third wheel which swivels. The seat is 19¾''–14¾'' wide, 14'' deep, 16'' high. The four-slat back is 47½'' high. The wheels are 21¼'' in diameter, held to the axles by linchpins; the eight delicately turned spokes are of maple, with oak rims; the entasis of the spokes has three delicate scribe marks for

30

31

decoration. The back wheel is of maple, 4¾″ in diameter, set into a sliding, adjustable block to regulate the angle of the back; the socket swivels. (Shaker Museum, Old Chatham, N. Y.)

29. Back view of the chair in Fig. 28. Both the adjustable back wheel and the large side wheels can be removed and the chair reconverted to a rocker. Note the enlargement of the legs just above the runner. The blunt-ended arm swells out enough to give a hint of the development of the side-scrolled arm.

30. Early armed rocker, New Lebanon. Side-scrolled arms supported by simply turned posts with button tops. Red mahogany stain, maple frame. (Private collection)

31. Detail of the side-scrolled arm of the rocker in Fig. 30.

32. Unusual five-slat rocker from Enfield, Conn. Other noteworthy features are the shape of the runners, with their unusually long horns, and the oversize yet graceful mushrooms. The proportions of the finials are not so happy, however; they are too

small and pinched-off for the massiveness of the posts. (Shaker Museum, Old Chatham, N. Y.)

33. Detail of the mushroom of the rocker in Fig. 32. This is quite the largest the author has ever seen; it measures 3⅛″ in diameter, but only ½″ in thickness.

34. Finial from the rocker in Fig. 32. Perhaps the unsatisfactory proportions stem from the fact that the taper below the finial proper is too like in size to the finial itself.

32

34

33

35

36

37

35. No. 7 armchair from Mt. Lebanon, the largest size sold. Elder Robert Wagan standardized the form of the finial and the arm with its domed mushroom. Stained logwood-red and varnished; woolen worsted tape seat. (Shaker Museum, Old Chatham, N. Y.)

36. Finial of the armchair in Fig. 35. This type of finial, devised and standardized by Elder Robert, continued to the end of the chair manufacturing, and is characterized by the acorn shape and tight, pronounced neck.

37. Mushroom of the armchair in Fig. 35. These mushrooms had a fairly high dome, and were attached to the peg-top of the front post, which extended a half-inch through the arm. Note that the mushroom did not extend over the arm piece.

38. Hancock armed rocker, c. 1890. Hancock armed rockers and armchairs were notable for the proportions of the seat,

and for the mushrooms and finials, derived but differing from the contemporary Mt. Lebanon model. The seat is 20½″–18″ wide, 20″ deep, and but 12¾″ high; the arms are 10⅝″ above the seat. The back also has four slats; these are quite narrow, with a pronounced widening in the middle. Oddly enough, the unusually high arms are not uncomfortable in use. (Cf. the proportions of the Mt. Lebanon counterpart, Fig. 35.) Chestnut; dark brown stain and varnish. Hancock chairs were not given a model number or identifying decal, as at Mt. Lebanon. (Private collection)

39. Finial of the rocker in Fig. 38. While similar to the Mt. Lebanon type, the acorn is bulbous and not pointed; the neck is shorter and less graceful (cf. Fig. 36).

40. Mushroom of the rocker in Fig. 38. Markedly flatter than the Mt. Lebanon variety, it is smaller than the width of the arm, and has edge turning (cf. Fig. 37).

39

38

40

41

43

42

41. Photograph taken in 1929 of the chair display room at the South Family, Mt. Lebanon, showing Sr. Sarah Collins and two sons of a hireling. Sr. Sarah supervised the making of all these chairs, and seated all of them personally, besides making all the rugs, quilts, spreads, etc. Note the spindle-back rocker (back row, center), and the tall-seated chairs with elongated finials, as well as the knob-topped "dining" chair in the lower left corner. This is indisputable proof that these chairs were made at Mt. Lebanon, although none appear in any chair catalogue. The carved-back Victorian Empire chair (back row, to Sr. Sarah's right) was also made at the South Family. (Private collection)

42. The Western Shaker communities produced a far greater variety of design than did the Eastern. Here we have a rush-bottomed side chair from North Union, Ohio. Not only is the finial very different from those of the North, but so are the legs, which exhibit the pronounced taper characteristic of chairs from Ohio to Texas. There are double scribe marks on the top of the front posts. (Western side chairs usually had four slats, also.) (Western Reserve Historical Society Museum, Cleveland)

43. Finial of the chair in Fig. 42. The double scribe marks are not necessarily peculiar to North Union.

44. North Union side chair, with a finial markedly reminiscent of Watervliet, N. Y. The legs, however, have the sharp mid-West taper which, with the four slats, differentiate the chair from Watervliet. The leather seat is old, if not original. (Western Reserve Historical Society Museum, Cleveland)

45. Finial of the chair in Fig. 44.

46. Two dining chairs from North Union. The one on the left is of rock maple, in the usual low-backed, two-slat form. That on the right, in curly maple, is much later, in a modified American Empire style. (Western Reserve Historical Society Museum, Cleveland)

46

45

44

47

48

49

50

47. Side chair from Union Village, Ohio. Patterned on a type common in the mid-West and far West, this has the usual four slats, here corner-notched, as the majority were. The back posts show a characteristic rabbit or mule-ear flattening, and the legs are sharply tapered. Unlike Northern construction, these slats are individually affixed at each end to the posts with two thin nails. (In the North a single wooden peg at the ends of the top slat sufficed.) The original finish featured cantaloupe-colored rounds and slats, and black posts. (Shaker Museum, Old Chatham, N. Y.)

48. Union Village armed rocker. Noteworthy are the splayed, five-slat, rabbit-eared back, and the broad scroll arms. The slats have the characteristic mid-Western corner-notching. The maple frame is painted black or very dark green. Much Western country furniture, Shaker and non-Shaker, is noted for its comparative massiveness, which borders on the clumsy. (Warren County Museum, Lebanon, Ohio; photo by Lees Studio, Chatham, N. Y.)

49. Armed rocker from Union Village. Noteworthy are the cyma-curved arms and the five-slat back, the slats of which become progressively wider as they rise from the seat, a characteristic of many Pennsylvania country chairs. Maple, varnished. (Warren County Museum, Lebanon, Ohio; photo by Lees Studio, Chatham, N. Y.)

50. Armed rocker from Union Village. Note the way the arms are supported, with terminal button-topped mushrooms. These arms are peculiarly ugly, ending as they do with a square rather than a rounded or scrolled section. The four slats are heavily corner-notched, and the finials have not yet received their Shaker design. (Warren County Museum, Lebanon, Ohio; photo by Lees Studio, Chatham, N. Y.)

51. Rocker from Pleasant Hill, Ky. Maple frame and cherry arms. Unlike most Northern Shaker chairs, this has only one front stretcher, not two. The side-scrolled arms are without mushrooms, and the finials are

51

club-shaped, somewhat suggestive of one design from Sabbathday Lake. (Shaker Museum, Old Chatham, N. Y.)

52. Detail of the rocker in Fig. 51, showing the way the arm is held to the post—cut flush and wedged. The scroll is unusually wide, also.

53. Finial of the rocker in Fig 51. Unlike the more conservative Northern communities, those in Kentucky especially seemed much less dedicated to a particular finial pattern, and used a considerable variety.

53

52

55

54. Slipper rocker from Pleasant Hill, originally a straight chair but made into a rocker by applying runners. To make the seat of the chair the proper height, the original straight legs were cut down somewhat before the runners were added. Note the urn finials and sausage turnings on the posts, most atypical features. (Shaker Museum, Old Chatham, N. Y.)

55. Finial from the rocker in Fig. 54. The varnished finish has alligatored and beaded with age. The back is pegged through only the top slat.

56. Rocking chair from Pleasant Hill. Maple frame. The excessive massiveness of this early piece is characteristic of those found in the West at this period. Noteworthy are the thick, corner-notched slats and the runners stepped where they are pegged into the legs. (Shakertown at Pleasant Hill, Inc.)

57. Loom chair, South Union, Ky. This has been contrived from an ordinary side chair by pegging the legs into a rather elaborate base constructed with a footboard. The chair is quite early, of maple, with massive legs. The back posts are bent and are of the rabbit-ear variety. The applied base seems later than the chair it supports. The seating is of very narrow splint. (Shakertown at South Union, Ky.)

58. South Union furniture. The desk has been constructed out of a one-drawer table; characteristic of the Western Shaker style is the elaborate turning on the legs. The chair at the left was heightened for use at the loom or ironing board by applying extenders called "boots" (not the patented tilter called by that name at New Lebanon); the original leg has the Western taper. The chair in the center has the common corner-notched slats, although this notching is deeper than usual. Since the chair has been cut down, one cannot tell if the legs were tapered, but it is probable. The loom chair at the back is interesting for the spaced spool-turning of the support for the dowel arm (a form of arm used in the North on relatively few documented Shaker chairs), and for the extreme style of taper on the legs. These finials are peculiar to Kentucky, and especially to South Union. The wood of all these chairs is maple. (Shakertown at South Union, Ky.)

59. Finial of a South Union rocking chair. This looks much like the stereotyped Mt. Lebanon finial of 1873 and later, except that it is appreciably larger, and also much earlier. This chair, of maple, probably dates from the 1830's. The strong arching on the slat marks the piece as Western, also. (Shakertown at South Union, Ky.)

54

56

57

59

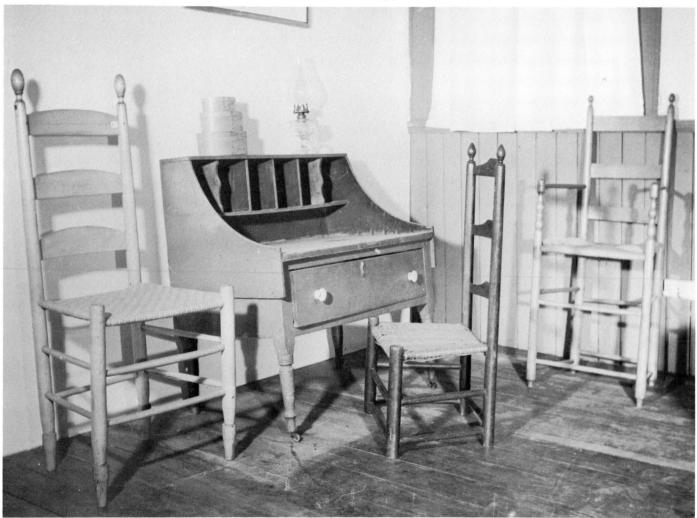

58

60

60. Armless rocker, South Union. The back posts have an outward splay, and the finials are of a type not found in the North. The slats are arched upward on both top and bottom, and each is pegged into the post. The seat is of woven cane. The runners are attached to the outside of the back legs and to the inside of the front legs, thus making them rock more nearly parallel to each other. Maple frame. (Shakertown at South Union, Ky.)

61. At the left, a South Union chair, painted yellow; only the front legs are tapered. The seat has been renewed. The chair at the right is probably from Watervliet, N. Y., and has tilters, a feature never found in the West. Natural finish, rush seat. (Shakertown at South Union, Ky.)

61

62. Two very early chairs, said to be Shaker, but of uncertain provenance. The rabbit-eared example is likely to be Shaker, the heavy side chair at the right almost certainly so. This illustrates the great difficulty encountered in trying to establish Shaker origins for pieces so nearly contemporary with non-Shaker prototypes. The earliest chairs, Shaker and Gentile alike, are usually very heavy and clumsy, due in large measure to the ignorance of the maker concerning the strength of the wood used, maple in this instance. (Kentucky Museum, Western Kentucky University, Bowling Green)

63. Two more very early country chairs, said to be Shaker but of uncertain provenance. Dowel arms are not uncommon on the earliest Shaker high chairs. The finials are distinctly reminiscent of Shaker ones, yet the sharp points give one distinct pause. Probably *not* Shaker, but contemporary World's chairs. (Kentucky Museum, Western Kentucky University, Bowling Green)

64. Three children's chairs from Canterbury. All are slab-seated; the little rocker on the right is very early, as can be seen in the form of the runners and the proportions of the back. Dimensions are as follows. Left-hand chair: 26″ high at back, 14″ at seat, which is 12⅝″–12″ wide, 13″ deep, 1-13/16″ thick. Center chair: 22-5/16″ high at back, 9⅞″ at seat, which is 12⅞″–12⅛″ wide, 13⅛″ deep. Right-hand chair: 22¼″ high at back, 12″ at seat, which is 13⅝″ wide, 14″ deep, and decidedly hollowed to fit the body. (Shaker Museum, Old Chatham, N. Y.; photo by Lees Studio, Chatham, N. Y.)

62   **63**

64

65

65. Two children's chairs. At the left, a Mt. Lebanon No. 0: back, 23" high, seat, 7½" high, 12¼"–10½" wide, 10¼" deep, replaced splint bottom. Black finish, imitating ebony. At the right, a Harvard baby's chair: back, 16¼" high; seat, 7¼" high, 9"–8" wide, 8" deep. Tape replaced. (Private collection)

66. Three children's chairs. Left and right, Mt. Lebanon: No. 0 at the left, with cushion rail; No. 1 at the right, armchair type. Center, three-slat settee, probably from Canterbury; dowel arms, characteristic of very early Canterbury pieces. Dimensions: No. 0: back, 23" high; seat, 8⅛" from floor. No. 1: back, 28⅞" high; seat, 10⅞" from floor. Settee: back, 24" high; seat, 25½" long in front, 23" in back, 7" high from floor, 10" deep. Very narrow splint seating. (Shaker

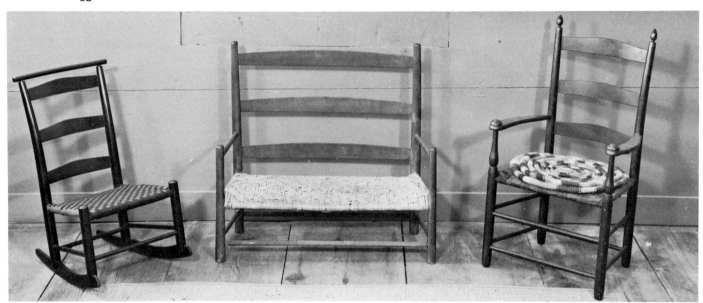

66

67

Museum, Old Chatham, N. Y.; photo by Lees Studio, Chatham, N. Y.)

67. Chairs from Mt. Lebanon. Left-hand chair: No. 1, 29½" high at back, 12" at seat. Center chair: No. 0 rocker, 23" high at back, 8⅛" at seat. Right-hand chair: No. 6 rocker, 43½" high at back, 16" high at seat, which is 21" wide and 18" deep. The child's table is made from an old drawer front complete with keyhole; it is 41-1/16" long, 15-9/16" wide, ½" thick, and 13⅜" high. To make it into a table, end cleats were applied and four delicately turned legs inserted therein. The No. 0 and No. 6 chairs were both included in this one picture to show the relative sizes of the smallest and next to the largest in the same model. (Shaker Museum, Old Chatham, N. Y.; photo by Lees Studio, Chatham, N. Y.)

68. Mt. Lebanon high chair, one of six made for special friends in 1880. It is noteworthy for its extreme grace and delicacy. The footboard has been restored and the legs extended five inches to the original

length (all but one chair had been cut down by their owners, either to lower them to the height of the table, or out of fear that an over-active child would tip himself over. (The baby was tied in with a spare diaper!) Maple, with a mahogany finish; half-inch red and black woolen worsted tape in a checkerboard pattern Height of back posts, 36"; of front posts to top of mushrooms, 32"; height of seat, 25", and of footboard, 19⅛". Seat is 12¼"–10½" wide, 10¼" deep. (Shaker Museum, Old Chatham, N. Y.)

69. Selection of South Union chairs. Clockwise, they are as follows. Ironing chair; maple; two-slat; high rush seat to allow use at the ironing board. Child's high chair with a pronounced splay to the front legs to assure freedom from tipping over; oddly enough, there are no upper stretchers at sides and back; splint seat. Child's high chair, more sturdily built and with arms; splint seat. All these chairs have the sharply tapered legs characteristic of the West, and finials very different from those in the North. (Shakertown at South Union, Ky.)

68

69

71

70. Children's furniture, largely from Kentucky. Twins' cradle is from Pleasant Hill, of pine, stained red. Length, 57"; width, 16"; height, 22½"; rockers are 22" long. The tiny bentwood rocker bears this tag in old handwriting: "Chair made by the Shakers before 1882. This is exact model of chairs made by Shakers [at Mt. Lebanon] now in use." It might have been a salesman's miniature sample, or a display sample. Height at back, 14¾"; of seat, 5½"; width of seat, 8¼"–6¾", and depth, 6¾". The larger bentwood would correspond to a Mt. Lebanon No. 3, although neither bentwoods nor spindle-backs were ever numbered or decaled. The Pleasant Hill high chairs, one with splayed armposts, are 34¼" high at the back; the seats are 20" high, 13½–11" wide and 10¾" deep; the front posts are 26½" high. The frames are of maple. The shoe-footed towel rack is from Pleasant Hill, and is heavier than Northern ones. (Shakertown at Pleasant Hill, Inc.; photo by Lees Studio, Chatham, N. Y.)

71. A "revolver," or swivel chair, from Canterbury. A variant of this form had heavy wire spindles instead of wooden ones. These chairs are said to have originated at Enfield, for use in schoolrooms, although other communities later made them. The slab seat is supported by a cast-iron, four-armed crowfoot attached to a steel rod; earlier types had a heavier wooden doughnut support screwed to the seat and support-

70

ing a heavy maple dowel. The Shaker term "revolver" seems to have been responsible for a journalist's wild story, found in an unidentified newspaper clipping of 1918, that the Brethren invented the Colt revolver! Pine, with maple standard. The seat is 14¾" in diameter, and 18½" from the floor; this height is adjustable. The comb back is 9¾" high. This form seems ultimately derived from the Windsor chair. (Shaker Museum, Old Chatham, N. Y.)

72. Comb-back, slab-seated bench of a type said to have originated at Enfield. Found in several communities, notably Canterbury, whence this came; it may have been brought to Canterbury from Enfield, or made there after the Enfield pattern. Seat is of pine, 49" long and 14" wide, and 16¼" high; height to the top of the back is 31". The legs and stretchers are of maple; the whole bench is natural-finished. Noteworthy is the lack of a longitudinal stretcher, which produces a certain amount of structural weakness. Some benches of this type had spindles bent gracefully, instead of straight ones as in this example. (Shaker Museum, Old Chatham, N. Y.; photo by Lees Studio, Chatham, N. Y.)

73. Group of Mt. Lebanon footstools, the only other type of furniture commercially produced for sale to the public. The two plank-topped stools in the foreground have the identifying decal under the top (although this is often omitted); the one on the right has a "shag" cushion in orange with a brown border. Those in the background illustrate some of the variations on the theme; the center one has the decal wrapped around one leg; the others lack this. (Shaker Museum, Old Chatham, N. Y.)

74. Interesting plank footstool from South Union, made of cherry, and dated 1803. Size, 18½" long, 10⅞" wide and 11¾" high. The stretcher is keyed at the ends by a long key or wedge inserted into the top. (Shakertown at South Union; photo by Lees Studio, Chatham, N. Y.)

72

73

74

75. Identifying decal used by Elder Robert M. Wagan at Mt. Lebanon after 1873 to mark those chairs and footstools manufactured by the South Family. Here applied, as generally with rockers, to the inside of a runner; it bears the model number, 1, which was usually also stamped on the back of the top slat, if the chair was so equipped. The decal was in gold. (Shaker Museum, Old Chatham, N. Y.)

76. Decal applied to the back of the bottom slat of an armchair. This was usual on armchairs, as well as on children's chairs (Nos. 0 and 1) when the runner was too narrow to accommodate the trade mark. Note the incorrect plural! (Shaker Museum, Old Chatham, N. Y.)

77. Decal wrapped around the post of a footstool. The model number (here, 0) was generally removed when the decal was applied to footstools, as these pieces of furniture were never model-numbered as were the chairs. (Shaker Museum, Old Chatham, N. Y.)

78. Decal applied to the bottom of a plank-topped footstool. Many footstools of this type lack the decal for some reason. (Private collection)

75

76

77

78

79

80

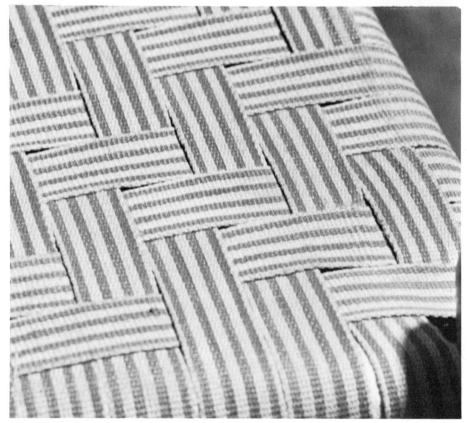

81

79. Webbing used in chairs. This was the original, handwoven type, found in a Canterbury rocker dated 1805(?). It is woolen, ¾" wide, and of a pleasant blue-gray, with an interrupted red thread-stripe near the edges. The numeral 5 stamped on the post was, according to Andrews, the last digit, or pair of digits, of the year; for this chair, [180]5. Considering similar numerals on other chairs, it seems more probable that such a numeral represented not the year but the number of the room where it was supposed to be used. (Shaker Museum, Old Chatham, N. Y.)

80. Second period of taping. Around 1850 and for some decades thereafter the Shakers found it more economical to buy machine-made tape for their chairs, as in this example. It was woven in woolen worsted in a twilled pattern, ½" wide. The Shakers bought it in white and dyed it to their specifications at home. This particular example is in tan and maroon in the checkerboard pattern. (Shaker Museum, Old Chatham, N. Y.)

81. Third and current period of taping, making use of cotton canvas webbing. The cotton tapes the Shakers used immediately following their abandonment of woolen worsted was of a very fine weave; later, as here, it became coarser. This is the type currently obtainable. The tape shown in this picture is probably early twentieth-century, and is a replacement of an earlier seat. (Shaker Museum, Old Chatham, N. Y.)

82. The photograph shows the number 19 stamped into the top of a front post. As was mentioned earlier, this may have been a date, and if so, this chair was made in 1819. Occasionally the full date is used. Sometimes we find such digits as 08, which could hardly refer to a room, but must be [18]08; in the case of double digits such as 19, the point is moot. The tape, incidentally, is of the transitional cotton type mentioned in the preceding caption; it is very fine and smooth, unlike the later, coarse canvas webbing. (Shaker Museum, Old Chatham, N. Y.; photo by Lees Studio, Chatham, N. Y.)

83. Benders for shaping the back posts of Mt. Lebanon chairs made in the 1890's, and for spindles in the "revolvers." The steamed or soaked post was carefully positioned with regard to slat-mortises and stretcher-holes, and then thrust finial-first under the strap metal collar at the right, squeezed down by hand into the shaper-groove, and the leather strap collar slipped over the free end. The post or spindle was then allowed to dry thoroughly before removal and assembling. (Shaker Museum, Old Chatham, N. Y.)

82

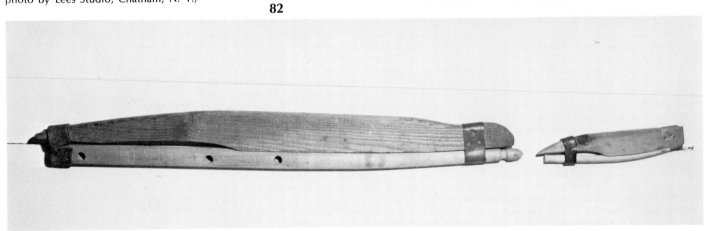

83

84

85

84. Room setting in a Shaker community, probably Hancock, c. 1935. From left to right we see the following; Pedestal desk in tiger-stripe maple, with snakefoot base and bone key escutcheon; a maple armless rocker; candlestand in rock maple stained cherry, with a snake-foot base; a chest-on-cupboard in pine; an early rocker with cushion rail and side-scrolled arms; a side chair with a light yellow stain; a stove with wrought iron legs ending in "penny" feet; and two circular, knitted rugs. (Shaker Museum, Old Chatham, N. Y.; photo by Lees Studio, Chatham, N. Y.)

85. Museum gallery setting. Seen in the photograph are two five-slat Enfield, Conn., rockers, a maple sewing desk from Sabbathday Lake, a mirror and mirror hanger from Hancock, a cherry drop-leaf table with one drawer from New Lebanon, a maple bed with trundle from New Lebanon, and a cupboard-on-chest from the same community, stained red, and supplied with a small two-step ladder to facilitate getting into the upper drawers and cupboards. (Shaker Museum, Old Chatham, N. Y.; photo by Lees Studio, Chatham, N. Y.)

86. Museum gallery setting. Principal pieces, left to right, are: Mt. Lebanon No. 4 rocker made into a sewing chair; cupboard-on-chest in pine, Watervliet, N. Y.; oval tripod table in maple, probably of late date, from Mt. Lebanon, snake-foot, and with two-plank top held together underneath by inset butterfly splines; sewing desk of mixed woods, chiefly maple and butternut, from Canterbury, c. 1890; children's chairs, Nos. 0 and 1, Mt. Lebanon. (Shaker Museum, Old Chatham, N. Y.; photo by Lees Studio, Chatham, N. Y.)

87. Museum gallery setting. Principal pieces, left to right, are: Secretary-on-chest, pine, New Lebanon, very early; dining table with splayed legs, butternut, late Canterbury; snake-foot candlestand, maple, New Lebanon; small desk, butternut, New Lebanon; five-drawer work table, pine with ivory inset escutcheons, Hancock. Chairs: Mt. Lebanon spindle-back; four-slat Mt. Lebanon rocker (in corner); rocker with turned posts (center foreground), Pleasant Hill; four-slat rabbit-ear side chair, Union Village. The braided rugs, 9' x 12', are both Shaker. (Shaker Museum, Old Chatham, N. Y.; photo by Lees Studio, Chatham, N. Y.)

86

87

2. TABLES AND DESKS

As was pointed out earlier, practically all sorts of Shaker furniture at the beginning either copied Worldly pieces, or were derived from or influenced by them. Tables were no exception. These exhibit considerably more variation in form, use and type than do chairs, and, like all Shaker furniture except chairs and footstools, were never produced for sale to the World. Occasional pieces might be made on special order for particular friends, but the Believers never went into a Grand Rapids type of production. As a consequence, there was not the incentive to bend to public whim in making "popular" pieces, either in form or design.

One of the oldest table types found in the New World was the sawbuck or X-leg table. It does not, however, constitute a common form. Some Shaker specimens still exist; they are, for the most part, of very early date.

By all odds the most usual was a simple pine table with four square tapered legs, derived from what is called Country Chippendale. A variant of this was a table with legs that were lathe-turned round below the skirting. Because of the close similarity with non-Shaker tables of the same types, it is often extremely difficult and not infrequently impossible to tell which is Shaker and which is not. Very often a purchaser will have pointed out to him the dovetailing, or the fact that a piece is "in the old red paint," as proof of Shaker origin. Sad to relate, all non-Shaker cabinetmakers of the nineteenth century dovetailed, and generally extremely well; the "old red paint" was very common indeed on most country pine furniture. Further, by no means did the Shakers always dovetail their drawers and corner joints; plenty of examples exist of simple nailed points, rabbeted or otherwise. (The nails, by the way, were usually square cut-nails; handwrought nails are seen on only the very earliest pieces and then seldom; and wire nails rarely even on those pieces made in the twentieth century. When found, they generally indicate either modern repairs ineptly made, or a reproduction.)

Another misconception easily exploded is the myth that the Shakers always pegged their furniture. Generally speaking, all but the earliest pieces used both nails or screws, often in considerable abundance, the most common exception being in the corners of table frames and the door stiles of cabinets; on these the use of pegs continued until quite late.

How, then, can one be sure whether the simple, square-tapered-leg pine table, which one is asked a high price for, is Shaker or not? First, by knowing one's dealer, who, if he is reputable, will say from what area the piece came, and will often indicate from what community. He will stand behind his merchandise and will not state authoritatively that a piece is Shaker if it is certainly not, or if it is doubtful. But one must remember that he, like museum directors and dedicated, long-time collectors, can be in honest error—which is the reason for the writing of the present book; the same consideration animated Dr. Edward D. Andrews in writing *Shaker Furniture* and *Religion in Wood*. Second, one must consult photographs of known pieces and use one's own intelligence and experience. There is no collector or dealer who has never made an error; we must all, unhappily, learn by our own mistakes. It is the hope of the author that this volume will help reduce the margin of error.

The earliest furniture generally did not mix woods; a table or bench was *all* maple or pine or cherry; as time went on, it was increasingly common to find a mixing of woods, such as a maple base and cherry top. Many late pieces, such as some of the sewing desks, used six or more woods in differing places and for differing effects.

For many types of furniture, various communities tended to produce variations on a theme by which one is helped to identify the source. For instance, the Maine communities, especially Sabbathday Lake, frequently turned button feet on the bottoms of table legs. Three Northern communities were well known for furniture distinctly more elaborate than their neighbors': Enfield, Connecticut; Enfield, New Hampshire; and Watervliet, New York. Of these, Enfield, Connecticut ("Old Enfield"), departed farthest from the norm. Furthermore, some communities produced forms evidently not found elsewhere, such as the tip-top tripod tables, made in Alfred and Sabbathday Lake, Maine, and Harvard and Shirley, Massachusetts.

Dining tables were quite generally of the trestle variety. They consisted of a plank top with breadboard ends to prevent warping (by no means an exclusively Shaker feature), supported by two or three pedestal trestles, these in turn resting on a flat shoe-foot or arch-foot base. This style of table required no skirted frame, and thus gave more leg room; it also allowed the low-backed dining chairs to be slid beneath and got out of the way. Parenthetically, chairs were never put at the ends of the table as is customary with us today; the ends were left open for service.

Candlestands, and their derivatives, sewing stands, were made in each community. Generally of maple or cherry, or both, they were of the pedestal type. The earliest had peg-feet; later ones had snake-feet (the ogee version of the elaborate Queen Anne foot) or spider-feet (a simple arched type, and probably the earlier of the two).

These above-mentioned varieties were only a few of those made by Believers to supply their needs. Work tables for kitchen and wash shops, dressmakers' tables, occasional tables, night stands, shop pieces—the variety is manifold. Those of the North were generally equipped with tapered square legs (the taper almost always on the two inner sides), or turned round ones, generally with no secondary turnings thereon. Those of Ohio and Kentucky, more often the latter, are markedly elaborate, influenced without doubt by the plantation furniture so common in the South. Also, the proportions are for the most part decidedly heavier, often to the point of clumsiness, as compared with Northern pieces.

Table tops were occasionally pegged through into the frames, though much more commonly affixed thereto by screws put diagonally up through the skirting. On tables, mortises were blind—that is, did not run through, exposing the end of the tenons. Breadboard ends seldom were flush with the sides of the top—indeed, seldom should have been. Wood, even long- and thoroughly seasoned wood, always moves, expanding in damp weather and contracting in dry. Soft woods are naturally more prone to this process than hard. If the breadboards are fixed firmly to the ends of the top, the planks of the latter cannot move as they swell, and the wood splits. These breadboard ends, therefore, have screw or peg holes slightly oval to accommodate this movement. Modern restorers, often not knowing this constructional feature, will fix their crosspieces firmly to the top, sometimes even gluing them in place—with disastrous results.

So-called Pembroke tables, with diagonal cross-stretchers, were not made by the Shakers; tavern tables, with very low stretchers going beltwise from leg to leg, were very rare; the writer has seen but two. Such stretchers markedly hamper the sliding in or out of chairs; further, Believers were taught not to cock their feet up on chair stretchers (both because this was considered bad manners, and because of wear), and tavern-table stretchers would naturally fall foul of the same stricture.

Many tables had a single drop-leaf; why only one and not two is unclear, unless because it required less moving of the table away from the wall to increase the working surface when not much of an increase was needed.

Desks were probably derived originally from tables and then were specialized for writing and storing of documents and supplies. Shaker desks took several forms: children's writing desks, school desks, accountants' desks, single and double trustees' desks, and small lap or table-top desks. Woods used varied widely, as did the forms: pine for the earliest; black and brown walnut and cherry (in the West particularly), maple, butternut, or combinations of these.

Most frequently desks were built on a frame supported by tapered square legs (in the North) or turned round ones (in the West). Some were made on a sort of divided chest, like our old-fashioned roll-tops, but lacking the roll-top type of upper section; one, possibly unique, was a bureau-desk, with the top "drawer" really a front lid that let down on brass quadrants at the sides to make the writing surface, with pigeonholes behind. Often a bookcase-secretary top was superimposed above the pigeonhole section, generally with closet doors to close it, but occasionally with open shelves. Those with glass-fronted doors seem to come from Watervliet, New York.

88

89

90

88. Reading stand in tiger-stripe maple with peg-legs. From Alfred or Sabbathday Lake. Despite its looks, this is not a candlestand, since the top slopes slightly to facilitate reading a book set thereon. The top measures 13⅝″ by 15⅝″, and is 27⅜″ from the floor at one end, and 26¾″ at the other. The three legs are set interestingly into an octagonal post and ingeniously pegged. When obtained by the Museum, the maple standard had been grained a tiger-stripe maple, as had the top. Since the finish was in very poor condition, it was found necessary to remove this graining— at which time it was discovered that beneath the graining the top was genuine tiger-stripe! The standard and legs are of rock maple. (Shaker Museum, Old Chatham, N. Y.)

89. Candlestand, New Lebanon. Maple, with a cherry top, the diameter of which is 19″. This top is 26″ high, supported beneath by a wooden "doughnut" 7½″ in diameter, into which the top of the threaded standard is screwed. (Shaker Museum, Old Chatham, N. Y.)

90. Underside of the candlestand in Fig. 89, showing the supporting "doughnut" into which the threaded standard is screwed. Not all such candlestands had the threaded standard; the others had the top of the post glued into the "doughnut." The snake-foot legs were dovetailed into the standard, and were then covered with a plate of thin sheet iron cut to the profile, and used both for reinforcing the joint and for covering it. This is not an exclusively Shaker device, but was commonly used by them, more especially in the North.

91. Candlestand from Union Village. An astonishing piece in very strongly marked tiger-stripe maple, with a varnished natural finish. The standard is quite elaborately turned, a characteristic of the West, and in marked contrast to Northern pieces. Dimensions: 27½″ high, 12¾″ top diameter, 20½″ spread to the legs. It is unusual for the top to be so small compared to this spread. (Warren County Museum, Lebanon, Ohio; photo by Lees Studio, Chatham, N. Y.)

92. Underside of the candlestand in Fig. 91. Note the "doughnut" and the interesting turned button covering the dovetailed joints of the legs. This has a concealing, not reinforcing, function, wherein it differs from the Northern sheet-iron contour plate.

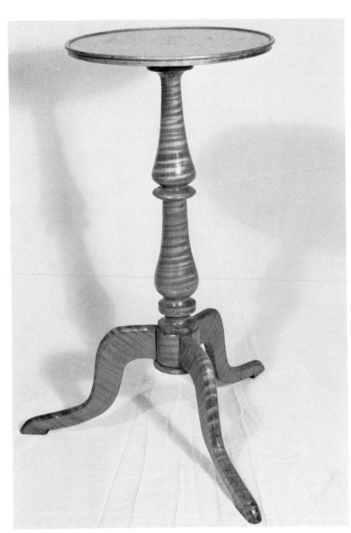

91

92

93

94

95

93. Cherry candlestand from Union Village. Noteworthy are the turnings of the standard, and the spider-feet, terminating in little pads rather reminiscent of the snake-foot leg, but much straighter and heavier. Height, 26½''; diameter of top, 17''. (Warren County Museum, Lebanon, Ohio; photo by Lees Studio, Chatham, N. Y.)

94. Candlestand from South Union, made for and used by Eldress Jane Cowan. Cherry, 28¾'' high, with a top 17½'' in diameter. The snake-foot legs are unusually delicate for Western furniture. (Kentucky Museum, Western Kentucky University, Bowling Green; photo by Lees Studio, Chatham, N. Y.)

95. Construction details of the candlestand in Fig. 94. The pedestal is threaded at the upper end and screws into the cleat-base of the top. The legs are dovetailed into the standard, but lack the covering sheet-iron reinforcing plate common to such tables in the North. (Photo by Lees Studio, Chatham, N. Y.)

96. Candlestand from Union Village. Cherry. Note that the snake-foot legs are much thicker than their Northern prototypes, as is the top. The standard is both heavier and much more elaborately turned than those of the North as well. Height, 27''; diameter of top, 16''. (Warren County Museum, Lebanon, Ohio; photo by Lees Studio, Chatham, N. Y.)

97. Corner of room in the Center Family dwelling, Pleasant Hill. All the furniture is from that community. The rocking chair has the heavily scrolled arms and corbeled runners which are characteristic of Kentucky, as are the rather elaborate turnings of the candlestand. The hanging wall sconce was designed for two candlesticks. (Shakertown at Pleasant Hill, Inc.)

96

97

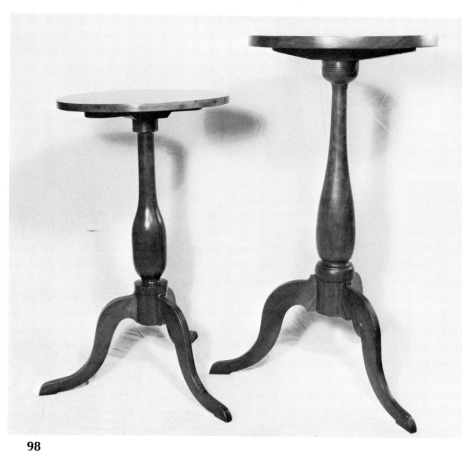

98

98. Tripod tables from South Union. The one at the left is of cherry, 28″ high, with a top 16¼″ in diameter. The bottle-shaped standard comes very close to being clumsy. The top has a cleat support. The table at the right is a book stand, used in the meetinghouse to support the Bible which was read in meeting; it was thus a sort of lectern. Of cherry, it is 33½″ high, with a top of 17½″ in diameter, supported by a cleat. Noteworthy is the thickness of the top, a full inch, quite common in Kentucky tables (cf. Figs. 104 and 105). (Shakertown at South Union, Ky.; photo by Lees Studio, Chatham, N. Y.)

99. Two stands from South Union. The one at the left is unusual for two reasons: the snake-foot legs have a wider splay than is customary, and the top is oval, a very rare form for this sort of table. Curly maple. The top measures 14⅜″ by 10¾″; the height is 24½″. Because of its shape and height, it was probably used as a chair-side book stand. (Private collection) The table at the right is the usual candlestand, but with the unusually thick top frequently found in Kentucky; it is 11¾″ in diameter, and is supported by a wooden "doughnut." Height, 23½″. Noteworthy is the elaborate turning of the pedestal, and the block support for the peg-legs. The wood is either chestnut or ash, both of which were Kentucky furniture woods. The large knob attached to

99

the baseboard of the wall was used as a doorstop or bumper. (Shakertown at South Union, Ky.)

100. Tip-top table from Harvard. Maple, with a snake-foot standard. The top is an early Shaker replacement in butternut of an original, probably two or three inches larger in diameter; the reason for the replacement is not clear. Present diameter of top, 24"; height, 27⅝". (Shaker Museum, Old Chatham, N. Y.)

101. The table in Fig. 100, with top raised. Tables of this type were, according to Dr. Edward D. Andrews, made only in Maine, and at Harvard and Shirley. Those in Maine, such few as are known, seem to have been locked in the down position with the brass catches common to tables of this type made by the World. The locking mechanism of this Harvard table is much simpler and more secure —simply a peg run through the top of the standard and the two bracing pieces of the top, and parallel to the hinge peg. The locking peg is here shown drawn part way back. Height to top of post, 27⅛".

102. The table in Fig. 100, with locking peg in the lock position. Only five Shaker tip-tops are currently known; they were used originally in the Sisters' shops and bedrooms (known as retiring rooms by the Believers).

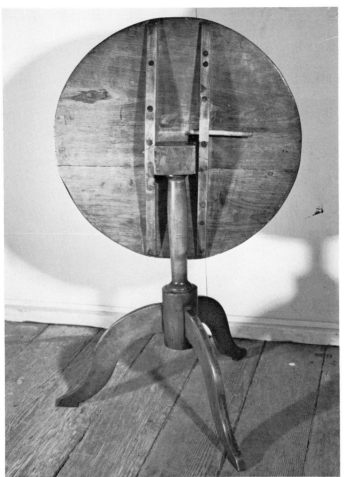

101

100

102

103

104

103. Two pieces from Canterbury, with a clear varnish finish. The small rocker in curly maple is made over from a straight chair, probably originally furnished with tilters. (See also Fig. 233, center.) Early nineteenth century. Seat, 11¾″ from the floor, 17⅜″–13¼″ wide and 12¾″ deep. Back posts, 37⅛″ high. Stamped on the top of the right-hand front post is "19," probably a room number, though it might be a date, [18]19. The small table has a tiger-stripe maple frame and curly-bird's-eye maple legs; there is one drawer at one end and two at the other, all with wooden knobs. Dimensions: top, 33⅞″ by 19⅛″, 9/16″ thick and 25¾″ high. (Shaker Museum, Old Chatham, N. Y.; photo by Lees Studio, Chatham, N. Y.)

104. Cherry side table from Pleasant Hill. As is common with Kentucky pieces, the top is very thick, measuring a full inch, while the drawer fronts are ⅞″ thick. The table is 33⅛″ long, and 15¼″ wide with the leaf down—25⅛″ with it up. It stands 29½″ high. Each end has a small drawer. Notable is the complete lack of any transitional shoulder between the square and round parts of the legs. (Shaker Museum, Old Chatham, N. Y.)

105. Detail of the table in Fig. 104, showing the wall leaf up, and supported by the square support-slide with its delicately turned knob. The beautiful rule joint of the leaf edge is noteworthy.

106. Cherry button-foot table with one drawer, from South Union. Interesting is the transition of the tapered round leg from the square corner post of the frame, with the simple turning below the collar. Size, 32″ by 24½″ by 28″ high. Legs pegged into the table frame. (Shakertown at South Union, Ky.; photo by Lees Studio, Chatham, N. Y.)

107. Two-drawer cherry side table from South Union. The turnings on the legs are interesting. Size, 28″ by 19½″ by 28¾″ high without the casters, which seem to have been added later. Again, note the massiveness characteristic of Kentucky pieces. (Kentucky Museum, Western Kentucky University, Bowling Green.)

106

107

105

108. Table from South Union. Golden ash frame, maple legs, cherry top. Most interesting is the fact that the drawer front is cut out of the skirting of the frame; note that the grain continues that of the frame itself. Size of the top, 46¼" by 20" by 1" thick; it is 27¾" high. The legs have the sharp taper characteristic of the West. (The "N.F." on the basket signifies "North Family.") (Shakertown at South Union, Ky.)

109. Gallery setting. Entrance Hall, Shaker Museum, Old Chatham, N. Y. Left to right: 16-drawer chest of drawers from New Lebanon, pine, stained red; two-drawer blanket chest from New Lebanon, pine, chrome-yellow stain; cherry wardrobe, Pleasant Hill, natural finish; 16-drawer tailor's bench from New Lebanon with removable top, pine, natural finish; 11-foot maple dining table, Hancock, with three trestles, dark stain; drop-leaf miniature wild cherry table from Hancock, maple frame, natural finish; Fountain Stone from Groveland, used in outdoor religious services in the 1840's; corner of accountant's desk, cherry, from Pleasant Hill. (Shaker Museum, Old Chatham, N. Y.; photo by Lees Studio, Chatham, N. Y.)

110. Dining table from South Union. Walnut top, ash trestles. The top is unusual in that the thirteen planks making it up run crosswise of the length, a feature seemingly found only at South Union. Dimensions: 8'9" long, 37½" wide, 28" high. (Shakertown at South Union, Ky.)

111. Dining table and chairs, Pleasant Hill. The table has very heavy trestles and gives the feeling of massiveness, even clumsiness, very different from the Northern versions. Butternut. Dimensions: 70" long, 41½" wide, 28½" high. While the dining chairs have the traditional low back, they are still not low enough to go entirely under the

108

109

table top as in the North. (Shakertown at Pleasant Hill, Inc.)

112. Side view of the dining table pictured in Fig. 111, showing constructional details. The top is made of four wide planks running lengthwise, unlike those at South Union. To be noted also is the turning on the posts and front stretchers of the chairs.

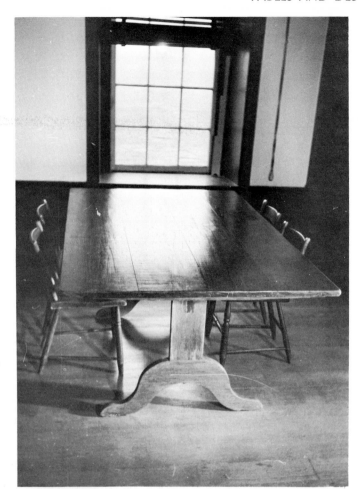

110

111

112

113

114

113. Dining table, New Lebanon. This variety with the tapered square legs, a form of the "country Chippendale," is quite typical of one type of dining table found in the North, the other being the trestle table. Pine, natural finish. Dimensions: 9'1/2" long, 333/4" wide, 281/2" high, with breadboard ends. (Shaker Museum, Old Chatham, N. Y.)

114. Particularly elegant dining table from Canterbury, from the Ministry dining room. Made by Elder Henry C. Blinn. Of butternut, it has delicately turned legs that splay outward from the center. Natural finish. The top, of two boards without breadboard ends, is 711/2" long, 311/4" wide, and stands 281/4" high. (Shaker Museum, Old Chatham, N. Y.)

115. Detail of the breadboard end of the table in Fig. 113. These cross-pieces, used to keep a single-plank top from warping, were never glued or nailed firmly in place in order to allow for the inevitable movement of the wood. If it were fastened firmly, when the top shrank in a dry period (as illustrated in this plate), the top would invariably crack. In the photograph, the breadboard end extends a full quarter-inch on each side beyond the top. Thus, in a top 24" wide, the dry-weather shrinkage is at least a half-inch in width. (The breadboard end is usual in much American furniture, especially that made of pine, where the movement is very considerable, even in old wood.) These ends should never be trimmed flush with the sides of the table, however great the temptation on the part of the tidy-minded.

116. Close-up of a so-called "rule joint," found on a wild cherry table from Hancock, seen in Fig. 109, right background. Note the closeness of fit, seldom found on rule joints used on non-Shaker furniture, and almost never on present-day ones.

117. Sewing desk from Canterbury, made in 1860 by Bro. Eli Kidder when he was 77. Pine, with a maple frame; the working surface is of bird's-eye maple, with a pine slide beneath to increase the work area. Dimensions: 243/4" long, 213/4" wide; the main section is 261/2" high. The upper section is 83/4" deep and 121/4" high. The pull-out slide has breadboard ends, and is 223/4" wide and 211/2" deep. (Shaker Museum, Old Chatham, N. Y.)

117

115

116

118

119

118. Sewing stand from New Lebanon (*left*), of maple. Note the delicately turned legs, not usual in the North. Dimensions: 31⅞" wide, 21⅞" deep, 28" high to working surface. The upper section, holding the drawers, is 30½" wide and 7⅞" deep; its top measures 31-5/16" by 8". The eight-drawer pine sewing stand (*right*) is from Canterbury, and is 13½" wide, 15⅛" deep, and 38⅜" high. The top drawer is fitted with pegs for holding spools of thread; the other drawers are for storage only. (Shaker Museum, Old Chatham, N. Y.)

119. Sewing stand from Watervliet, N. Y. Fairly late, it was used by Eldress Anna Case (1855–1938) of that community, and may well have been made for her; the casters and porcelain knobs are original. The working surface and top are equipped with a raised molding to keep things on them from rolling off. Dimensions: 21½" wide; overall depth, 21"; depth of working surface, 14"; height of the latter, 27½"; overall height at back, 40". (Shaker Museum, Old Chatham, N. Y.)

120. Sewing desk from South Union, made for Eldress Angeline Perryman, mother of Elder John Perryman. Curly maple and walnut. Hinged at either back corner of the spindle gallery is a bracket arm with heavy wire rods to hold spools of thread. One drawer and a sloping foot-rest. Size, 22¾" long, 15¾" wide and 22¾" high to the desk top. (Kentucky Museum, Western Kentucky University, Bowling Green; photo by Lees Studio, Chatham, N. Y.)

121. Two sewing desks from South Union. With their splayed, spidery legs they are in marked contrast to the case pieces of this type in the North, and seem to be a purely Kentucky form. At the *left* is a desk in cherry, with a pull-up spool drawer at the back, held in place by a wooden catch; it is shown in the closed position. There is a large, under-top drawer, with a pull slide below for additional work area. Noteworthy is the bow front of the top, with its low and delicate gallery at the sides and back. Size, 25¾" long, 18" wide and 25½" high. At the *right* is a desk in maple, with interestingly turned splay legs and stretchers of a type not seen in the North. The gallery rises at the back to a spool and implement rack. There is one narrow drawer, hung by the top edges of the sides. Size, 24¾" long, 12¾" wide and 24¾" high to the top of the working surface. (Shakertown at South Union, Ky.)

122. The left-hand sewing desk in Fig. 121, with the spool drawer released and raised; the catch now holds it in the "up" position.

120

122

121

123

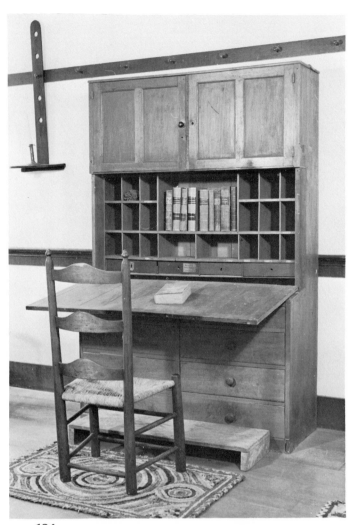

124

125

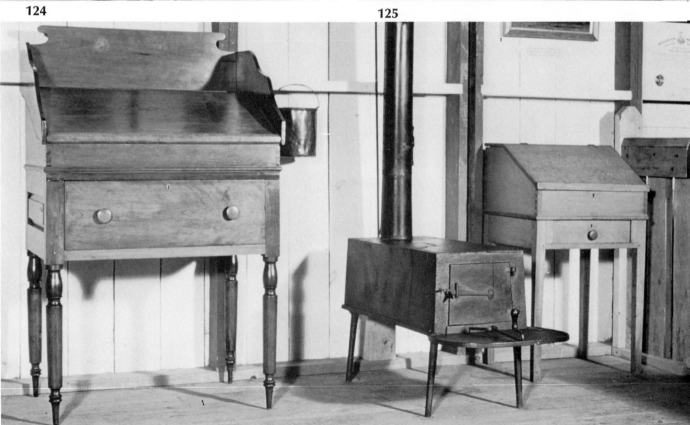

126

123. Tripod desk from Hancock, once in the bedroom used by a Church Family deaconess. This beautiful piece has a curly-maple base and pine top. The desk portion is 24½" long and 17¾" wide; there are no pigeonholes or trays built into the interior. To the top of the writing surface in front it is 24"; at the back, 27". The simple cavetto moldings are applied. (Hancock Shaker Community, Inc., Pittsfield, Mass.)

124. Early secretary-desk of pine, with a storage place for books at the top, and pigeonholes for papers below. The desk lid swings up to cover the pigeonholes when not in use. Probably from Pleasant Hill. Overall height, 71¼"; width, 45"; 17½" deep at the bottom, 13" at the top. The rather massive side chair is Pleasant Hill; note the finials and bow-topped slats. The two-candlestick sconce has the bow-topped hanger customarily found at Pleasant Hill. This type varied from 30" to 36" or more, with spaced holes for adjustment to differing convenient heights. Such long hangers were needed for rooms some of which were eighteen feet in height. (Shakertown at Pleasant Hill, Inc.; photo by Lees Studio, Chatham, N. Y.)

125. Desk of butternut ("white walnut" or "oilnut") with pine interior, from New Lebanon. Length, 35"; width, 22¼"; 27" to the top of the writing area at the hinge. The secretary section is 12⅜" wide and 20½" high. Natural finish. (Shaker Museum, Old Chatham, N. Y.)

126. Two desks of differing size and provenance, but of the same basic design. That at the left is an accountant's or trustee's desk from Pleasant Hill, and is of the stand-up variety. Of cherry, it has the elaborately turned legs and rather fancy gallery characteristic of Kentucky design, as well as deep side panels. It is 35¾" wide, 24" deep, 41¾" high to the front of the lid, and 49" to the flat area at the top. The gallery is 10⅜" high at the back and 7¼" at the sides. There is a shelf under the lid, but no pigeonholes. That at the right is a child's desk from Canterbury, in pine. The square legs are tapered in the country Chippendale tradition. The width is 22¾", the depth is 19¼", and the height is 34⅜" at the front of the lid and 41" at the back. The large stove is one of four used to heat the meetinghouse at Mt. Lebanon about 1830. (Shaker Museum, Old Chatham, N. Y.; photo by Louis H. Frohman, Bronxville, N. Y.)

127. Four-place school desk in pine, probably from Pleasant Hill, as are the other pieces. The wall cupboard above it is hung from the ubiquitous pegboard. Dimensions of the desk: 96" long, 29¾" high at the back and 26⅜" in the front; it is 20" deep. Each lid is 25" by 14½". It is finished in the common red paint. The wall cupboard, also in red, is 30¾" long, 19" high and 7⅛" deep, with top and bottom boards extending a half-inch beyond the sides. The bench, likewise red, is 71½" long, 7½" wide and 16½" high. (Shakertown at Pleasant Hill, Inc.; photo by Lees Studio, Chatham, N. Y.)

127

128

129

128. Accountant's or farm deacon's stand-up desk from Pleasant Hill. Of black walnut, it has square untapered legs, two drawers and a double lift-lid. The width is 67", the depth, 29¼"; it is 45¾" high at the front of the lid and 49½" at the back, with pigeonholes under the right-hand lid. (Shaker Museum, Old Chatham, N. Y.; photo by Louis H. Frohman, Bronxville, N. Y.)

129. Accountant's or trustee's desk from Pleasant Hill, of brown walnut. There are two drawers and a single large lift-lid, with no pigeonholes beneath. A gallery 6" high encircles the back. Width, 40½"; depth, 27"; height at front of lid, 43½", and 49½" to the flat part at the back. To the right, a "plantation desk," also from Pleasant Hill,

in cherry. The top is not attached to the table base, which is 47½" long, 20" wide and 35" high, with one drawer; the upper section has two shelves, and is 39" long, 13¼" deep and 46" to the top of the cresting, which is not demountable. The left-hand rocker is from New Lebanon; the right-hand one, from Pleasant Hill. The stool is a non-Shaker commercial product bought and used by the Shakers. (Shaker Museum, Old Chatham, N. Y.; photo by Louis H. Frohman, Bronxville, N. Y.)

130. Gallery setting at the Shaker Museum, Old Chatham, N. Y. Most of the furnishings are around 1840. At the left is a pine desk from Watervliet, N. Y., here used to hold china; the shelves were originally for books.

Beneath the shelves is a drop-leaf concealing pigeonholes; below this, a lift-lid concealing a storage space and more pigeonholes. Width, 46¼"; depth, 26¾"; height in front, 30¾", height 35¾" to back flat section; the shelves are 8¾" deep and 43¼" high. The top is set into molding on the desk section. Originally painted dark green. Center: trestle table from Hancock, 8' long, 34½" wide, 28" high; maple, with breadboard ends on the top. Far right: large pine chest of drawers from Watervliet, N. Y., 60" wide, 22" deep, 76" high; rose-red stain. The stove is one of the earliest and is from Canterbury; said to be late eighteenth-century. Center, pine tin closet, described in Fig. 135. (Photo by Louis H. Frohman, Bronxville, N. Y.)

130

132

131

131. Two benches and a desk. The desk, late nineteenth-century, is of butternut, and came from Canterbury; it once had a secretary-top, now missing. The lid, of the slant-top variety, is supported on two slides. While retaining many of the classical Shaker lines, this desk nevertheless betrays the inroads of Victorian decadence, especially in the panelled sides and lid, and in the missing secretary-top. The bench at the left, of pine, is from New Lebanon and was early used in the meetinghouse there. It measures 7' long, 9" wide, and 16" high, with shouldered braces. The one at the right is also from New Lebanon and is of pine. It is 68" long, 14⅜" wide, with a seat 15" high and a back 27⅜" high. It was evidently constructed for use with cushions, now missing. (Shaker Museum, Old Chatham, N. Y.)

132. Canterbury church bench of pine, first quarter of the nineteenth century. Detail, showing bracing. The shoulders on the triangular braces make it impossible for there to be any movement or racking. The end planks are let into a groove on the underside of the top plank, and are held in place by nails. (Shaker. Museum, Old Chatham, N. Y.)

3. CASE PIECES AND MISCELLANEOUS PIECES; PEGS AND PEGBOARDS

The term "case piece" covers an infinite variety of furniture: built-ins, chests, cupboards, wardrobes, work benches, counters, cabinets, bureaus, beds, blanket boxes, tailoring benches, sewing desks and tables, etc. The woods employed were of almost equal variety. As a rule, the best furniture woods available in a given locality were the ones used. The Northern communities used pine to a very large degree, with maple the next most popular. Butternut was used a good deal in later days, especially at Canterbury. Cherry, either alone or combined with maple, was found somewhat, though much more commonly in tables. Walnut was employed rather extensively at Groveland, New York, and in Kentucky and parts of Ohio—obviously because large stands of these trees were present. Cherry was very commonly employed in Kentucky, both because of its easy availability, and also in conformity with Southern tradition. The more elegant and exotic woods, like rosewood and mahogany, used from Federal days and even earlier in the World's furniture, were not employed by the Shakers. Neither did they use inlay (except for keyhole escutcheons) or veneer, insisting on the honesty and beauty of solid woods. The writer knows of but two pieces of veneered Shaker furniture out of the hundreds he has seen; there seems to be no logical reason for these mavericks.

The best and most knot-free stock was selected for cabinetry, carefully air-seasoned, and then worked up expertly. Mortises were almost never blind, but extended entirely through the stiles, and the butt end of the tenon was exposed. Not only is a run-through mortise easier to make than a blind one, but it is stronger. Yet it makes demands upon the craftsman: mistakes of fit cannot be disguised by glue or fill, for anyone can see if such errors have been committed.

Door stiles, whether for rooms or cabinet pieces, were pegged. Generally two such pegs were used in each joint, not ranged one above another (lest the holes should follow the grain), but staggered, the inner nearer the panel. Wide center stiles generally had four pegs, similarly arranged, the two inner being nearer together than the outer. Thus pegged, it was difficult for a door to sag. The enclosed panels were usually flat on the outside, chamfered on the inside. The inner edges of the stiles have sometimes only a beveled surface, but more often a quarter-round transition on the outside—not a quarter-round molding, but an edge rounded on the stile with a molding plane. So cleverly is this rounding done that it is often very difficult to discover whether the molding is cut out with a plane or is a separate piece bradded in place.

It is frequently stated by furniture experts that case pieces with plank sides are earlier than paneled pieces. In general this is probably true, yet we do find paneling on very early Shaker pieces. It is true, however, that for the most part mixed woods indicate a later piece. Such a mixture is seen in a tiger-maple chest of drawers from North Union, on which we find a cherry top and walnut knobs. An even more spectacular piece is a Canterbury sewing desk with rock-maple sides and frame, walnut ridged-moldings bordering the drawer fronts, butternut top, tiger-stripe-maple working surface, and pine slide; white porcelain knobs adorn the front. These two pieces date from the late 80's to the mid 90's.

Dovetailing, most carefully done, is found on early and smaller pieces, but larger furniture, like the tall chests of drawers, generally had sides nailed together with square cut-nails—on the very earliest pieces, with hand-wrought nails, although these are exceedingly rare. Pieces like blanket boxes and chests, in the very earliest days, used staple-hinges (and occasionally leather strap-hinges); far more common were wrought butt-hinges. Blanket boxes usually used offset butterfly-hinges with a long tongue on the lid. This was apparently not a Shaker design, delicate though it was, as such hinges are found on non-Shaker pieces as well; the Shakers of the North especially seemed to like them.

Early drawers usually had fronts with extended lips which, because they were thin and rather delicate, had a bad habit of splitting off. One is permitted to guess that this was the reason why later drawers fitted flush with the frame and were without lips. Very often, too, the earlier chests of drawers had dust-boards between the levels of drawers. Glue-blocks in the corners of frames and on the underside of drawers are a sign of late manufacture. Early drawer bottoms were chamfered and fitted into rabbets on the sides and fronts of the drawers; they often extended beyond the drawer frame at the back as a stop.

One of the abiding mysteries is the use of locks on doors and drawers. It would seem that Zion was not so trustworthy as could be hoped! When locks were provided they were the usual commercial cabinet types of the time, and were installed in the normal manner. In earlier days the Shakers attached to the outside of the drawer or door an escutcheon of bone or ivory, rectangular or diamond-shaped. Rarely was this of some other shape, and more rarely inlaid. Very often none at all was used. The later locks came with a metal inset rim-escutcheon.

Finishes varied with period and locality. In the North the pine furniture was either lightly oiled, or stained blue, red or yellow. (Blue was used as a stain only extremely rarely; the wood grain, showing through, was ugly.) Dark moss green was occasionally used; like the blue, it was almost invariably used as a paint and not as a stain. Red and yellow, in several shades, were found both as paint and stain. Hard woods were generally stained and then varnished. Western Shaker pine furniture made less use, apparently, of stains than did the North.

Because of the wide variety of uses to which these case pieces and miscellaneous pieces were put, the forms followed no easily defined categories. For example, wood boxes varied markedly in size and design. They were short and shallow, generally, if they were for kindling; if for larger stove-wood, deeper and much longer. Sometimes a kindling-wood shelf was built on top of a large stove-wood box. Other wood boxes were equipped with lids; some had removable towel-racks or storage compartments above. Very often delicately turned small knobs were inserted into the sides on which to hang dustpan and brush or other implements.

Hanging cupboards were generally small and depended from the pegboards, though occasionally quite large and imposing examples are found, like one at Pleasant Hill. In a private collection is one which is probably unique, from Enfield, Connecticut; it is a hanging *corner* cupboard with a glass-paneled door, the dimensions of which are 9″ by 12″, with two shelves inside.

Corner cupboards in the usual sense are nearly as uncommon, though they were rather a favorite form amongst the World's People and had been from very early Colonial days. Possibly their lack of popularity with the Shakers stems from the aversion of the latter to catercorner furniture. Twin full-size corner cupboards are found in the kitchen of the Hancock Church Family Dwelling, where they are built into place and are without doors; from the front edge of the shelf to the inner corner angle the depth is about 32″. One in the dining room of the Center Family Dwelling at Pleasant Hill was a later addition; instead of rising from the floor, the bottom of the cupboard rests on the rail surmounting the wainscoting.

Pie-safes are among the rarer Shaker forms. Such pieces were fairly common in early American homes until late in the nineteenth century; they were used to hold pastry safe from insects and yet allow air to circulate. Those in the North had plank sides and screened doors; the Shakers copied this design. In Kentucky they followed a pattern strongly reminiscent of the Pennsylvania German version, which has double doors and sides paneled with pierced tin. In the Shaker Museum at Auburn, Kentucky, there are two from the nearby South Union community; the earlier has the rough side of the piercing on the inside of the safe; the later, on the outside. It has been said that this reversal of piercing was due to the discovery that insects could get at the enclosed pastry if the panels were pierced inward, but were frustrated of entrance if these were pierced outward.

The wardrobe is also an uncommon form, and seems to be largely restricted to Kentucky, the Northern Shakers apparently preferring either to fold and put away clothing in large drawers (very often in great banks built into attic storage rooms in dwelling houses), or hung on open hangers—often of the three- or four-tier variety, a Shaker idea—in under-eaves attic spaces. In Kentucky regular wardrobes are found in a variety of woods, generally either cherry or walnut.

The Shaker tailors and tailoresses, in common with all such craftsmen, needed furniture with long, broad tops on which to spread out cloth for cloaks, suits and other clothing. These flat surfaces were accordingly made in different sizes, with ranks of drawers and/or closets beneath, generally of pine, but occasionally of maple. They might be stained in "the old red," or clear-finished.

Another frequently found type is the blanket chest. Purists differentiate between the blanket *chest,* which had a storage compartment at the top and one or two (rarely three) drawers below, and the blanket *box* with no drawers and built low. The latter, far more often than the former, had a built-in till compartment with a peg-hinged lid, found at one or both ends of the box. This blanket container was a form very common amongst the World's People also for centuries. But the blanket *chest,* occasionally found with a hanging drawer attached to the bottom of the frame, very seldom had a built-in till. The drawers found below the storage area naturally cut markedly into the depth of this compartment, which is probably the reason for the lack of popularity of the three-drawer model. Blanket chests were occasionally painted a dark moss green; more often, they were stained a chrome yellow or were plain-finished. They were also sometimes found in red, and very rarely in blue. Red paint was much more common on the blanket boxes. Both chests and boxes were much more common in the Northern communities than in the Western.

The drawers on blanket chests and similar pieces were, particularly in earlier days, dovetailed. Blanket boxes, also, were dovetailed on the corners, but larger case pieces almost never. The plank ends of blanket chests frequently had a half-moon cutout; they are also found with plank legs, the inner sides of which have an angle of about 15° from the vertical, running up to a horizontal skirting which is perfectly plain. Occasionally the end cutout is ogee in form, though this seems restricted to only a few of the Northern communities and even then the use is not consistent. Comparable Kentucky pieces generally have lathe-turned stubby legs a few inches in height.

A highly specialized form of chest, equally beautifully made, is the big carpenter's chest or box, generally elaborately fitted out to hold various types of tools used by the cabinetmaker. These are always dovetailed at the corners for greater strength, and quite often have cast-iron or hand-forged drop handles for ease in moving. All sorts of little drawers and sliding shelf-boxes are fitted into the interior.

A furniture design found almost exclusively in the West, especially in Kentucky, is the sugar chest. This is a form peculiar to the Southern states, although it is also found in mansions in the North (but very rarely in country homes). It is in essence a nearly square box with a hinged lid, set on legs of medium height. Those found in Kentucky are generally of walnut or cherry, and follow closely the pattern common in Virginia.

Dressers, or "bureaus," are not common in the North, but are quite usual in Ohio and Kentucky, where they are generally of cherry, and less frequently of walnut. A comparable piece of furniture found in the North is generally much taller, rising to a height of from five to nine feet. (Small movable stepladders were used to gain access to the upper sections.) These tall chests often have storage cupboards above the ranks of drawers.

The sewing desk or table was very essential to the Shaker seamstresses. If it had a pull-out slide to increase the working surface, it was generally called a "desk"; without slide, it was a "table." The Northern forms differed markedly from the Western. In the North, they almost invariably had ranks of drawers in graduated sizes—top, bottom and side—while the Western version was quite generally on slender legs, sometimes of the sawbuck type; it had one drawer or none, and a low gallery, often of the spindle sort. These tables were much smaller than their Northern relatives, and were much more delicate and elegant. In the North, a sewing desk was very often shared by two Sisters, one of whom used the left-hand upper rank of drawers and those in the front of the base, while her companion used the right-hand upper rank and the end drawers of the base. These desks were set on short legs, often simply turned.

Tin cupboards (for holding kitchen and dining room tinware or toleware) are an example of utilitarian work-pieces found in all nineteenth-century country homes, those of the Shakers not excepted. They were constructed of pine, severely plain, usually tall and narrow and with two doors concealing several shelves. Other types of cupboards of markedly varying forms were used in the infirmaries, printing offices, tailor's shops and other parts of the community. Very few pieces of Shaker furniture are either signed or dated; indeed, Ministry regulations expressly forbade using more than the maker's initials or the last two digits of the year, though by the 1830's these regulations were increasingly ignored; like the Soviets, the Shakers tried to avoid creating a "cult of individuality." Even so, with relaxed rules, few identifications or dates are found, and they are usually hidden on the bottom or sides of drawers, or in other arcane places. One tall clock case from New Lebanon had the maker's name and the date scrawled on the inside of the bonnet top; on another, the date and the maker's initials were discovered on the edge of the bedboard holding the movement and behind the overlapping dial!

The Shaker pegboards, while again not strictly furniture, are possibly the most characteristic and identifiable of all Shaker artifacts. Every room and every corridor, almost without exception, of every Shaker building was ringed with these all-purpose pegs, and if a given building is of doubtful Shaker provenance, a glance within (always assuming that interior reconstruction has not taken place) will, by the pegboards, tell surely whether or not it is of Shaker construction.

Before the days of cast-iron or steel hooks, the universal method of hanging clothing and other objects was the wooden peg, or occasionally a nail or spike. Our country ancestors of 150 years ago seemed not to have known of clothes hangers, or, if so, not to have used them. In those days, with few exceptions, country folk did not possess extensive wardrobes, so closets were not missed. Spare or Sunday clothes were either laid away in drawers or chests, or were hung on simple wooden pegs. Most coats, therefore, had peaks on the back of the collar.

The Shakers had a passion for neatness and tidiness, and abhorred clutter. There was an appointed place for everything, and everything was expected to be in its place. Very often the peg was that place. The pegboard, with its regularly spaced pegs (the spacing varied a good deal, according to the building, room and purpose), held all sorts of things: clothing (on hangers, be it noted—an improvement on non-Shaker custom!), brooms and mops, clocks, mirrors, small wall cupboards, certain tools, even straight chairs, which were frequently hung on the pegboards for storage or to clear the floor for cleaning.

Almost without exception, pegs made by the World's People were just that and nothing more, shaped by whittling or perhaps a draw-knife, and driven into a plank or beam. Occasionally they were more carefully made, with a small knobby head to help hold things from slipping off if the peg were not already driven in at a downward angle. Shaker pegs, however, were very different. They were invariably lathe-turned and graceful in form, terminating in a small mushroom, gently domed on the top. Smaller ones were occasionally used as drawer pulls. The wall pegs averaged about three inches in length, and were set in boards of about the same width, quite generally with a small, plane-molded beading on the edges.

Occasionally, and for special purposes, very much larger pegs were turned out. For instance, at Hancock gargantuan pegs were installed in the tan shop, apparently for hanging hides from the vats; of the same shape and proportions as the house pegs, these measured 13 inches in length! Similar ones were probably used for hanging harnesses in the stables, though few if any have survived.

Miniature pegs were set into what were called "sill boards," pegboards with stubby pegs fixed to the wall under the window sills. On these were hung dustpans and brushes, shears for the sister who might be doing a bit of private sewing by the window, or other small items. They were about an inch in length. Other miniature pegs, even smaller and more delicate, were often set into the sides of case pieces for particular uses, or beneath mirror hangers for comb and brush.

Pegs were generally turned out of maple and inserted into the boards, which were usually pine, and often painted a yellow ochre, although blue was universal in the meetinghouse. Occasionally other woods, such as walnut or cherry, were used for these boards; for example, the Shaker Museum at Old Chatham has one with both pegs and board in black walnut.

Particularly at New Lebanon, but also to a lesser degree at Hancock and Watervliet, about half the pegs were threaded and screwed into the boards;

the other half were friction-driven. This latter method seems to have been the universal custom in the rest of Shakerdom.

Most pegboards found in antique shops show a white line, more or less distinct, on the edges up to about half the thickness. The reason for this is interesting. When a building was erected, the Shakers affixed the pegboards directly to the lath, and plastered up to them on both sides. Seldom were these boards fixed on *top* of the plaster. If they are so mounted, it is an indication either that the Believers had installed them in a structure that they had not built, or that some non-Shaker had done the same thing. But built-in pegboards are a sure indication of Shaker construction. The dedicated collector, buying a length of pegboard, will leave this plaster-line as an indication of its provenance.

Since pegboards varied least in their design and construction between the various communities North and West, it has been thought unnecessary to include photographs of many examples. It is remarkable how closely pegs from various communities and from all periods resemble each other.

Akin to the pegs were the ubiquitous wooden knobs found on the drawers of Shaker furniture. They were of the usual mushroom type for the most part; throughout most of their history the diameter of the base skirting was the same as that of the mushroom top. The earliest, however, had a smaller top, and nearly skirtless stem. So common were these types all over early America, however, that one is often hard put to it to tell by looking at the knob only whether it is of Shaker manufacture or not. The Shaker ones are apt to be more delicate and more carefully made than those done by the World, but even this tenuous indication is far from positive.

Even though the Shakers not infrequently replaced broken or missing wooden knobs with white porcelain ones, they often installed such commercial pulls on a piece of newly made furniture. These can go back as far as 1840, so their appearance is not necessarily an indication of late and poor restoration. Fortunately, if such knobs need replacing by today's restorers, enough original ones can usually be found in most antique shops; they can also be obtained from companies engaged in making excellent reproductions. The same can be said of wooden knobs.

133

133. Very early New Lebanon sill cupboard or secretary on chest. Pine, natural finish. Overall height, 80"; lower section, 33" high; upper, 47". Width of lower section, 42¾"; upper section, an inch less; depth of the lower part, 18⅝", and of the upper, 10⅝". The upper section has many shelves subdivided into roughly square pigeonholes. The left-hand door has an ingenious Shaker-made spring catch operated by a short plunger pushed in on the right-hand side of the principal vertical divider. (Shaker Museum, Old Chatham, N. Y.)

134. Detail of cupboard door of the cupboard in Fig. 133. Part of the knob appears at the upper right corner, with the frame pegging below. The quarter-round molding bordering the inset panel is not a separate piece nailed into place, but is molded by plane on the edge of the stile; in this way, it is always in place and cannot lift or separate. The pegs of the door frame are inserted on a diagonal line, not vertically one over the other; this gives greater freedom from splitting of the stiles, and hence, greater strength.

135. Very early Watervliet tin cupboard, dating from c. 1810. Pine, natural finish. The upper section has one shelf; the lower, four, which are removable. Height, 82"; width, 21¾"; depth, 12½". This was almost certainly a built-in piece originally, and was used for holding tinware used in the kitchen or at the table. (Shaker Museum, Old Chatham, N. Y.)

135

134

136

136. Cabinet on chest, from Watervliet, N. Y. Pine, natural finish, c. 1830. Height, 72"; width, 40"; depth, 19⅝". One of the characteristics found on very many Watervliet case pieces is the molding generally found on the top, as well as the base, which is frequently more subtle and elaborate than on similar and contemporary Mt. Lebanon and Hancock furniture. Door panels, too, are very apt to make use of quite elaborate quarter-moldings, whereas Mt. Lebanon and Hancock pieces employ a simple quarter-round, generally made with a molding plane and not applied as a separate piece. (Shaker Museum, Old Chatham, N. Y.)

137. Detail of the latch on the door of the cabinet in Fig. 136. This "button," beautifully chamfered, is pegged to the shaft of a turnable knob on the other side of the door, and seats itself in a semilunar groove cut into the upper surface of a cupboard shelf. This latch is midway of the height of the door, with the shelf-line indicated by the cabinetmaker's scribe marks.

138. Detail of the vertical drawer divider of the cabinet in Fig. 136, showing the method of dovetailing into the frame. The horizontal dividers are similarly dovetailed into the sides. Note the wear on the drawer slides, and the scarring of the vertical divider caused by the lips of the drawers.

137

138

139. Three-door pine cupboard from the Church Family, Mt. Lebanon, c. 1820. The upper section has two shelves; the lower, three, vertically subdivided into large pigeonholes. Dimensions: 53¾" high, 31½" wide, 12¾" deep. Beaded (three-quarter-round) corners, done with a molding plane. (Shaker Museum, Old Chatham, N. Y.)

140. Double eight-drawer chest with closet space (the latter part with two built-in shelves). Watervliet, N. Y., c. 1830. Pine, with rose-red stain. 75½" high, 60" wide, 22⅜" deep. Watervliet pieces were generally finished with a top molding of some sort; here, a projecting plank top with square molding applied beneath, and with another, thinner plank above, well inside the major part of the top. (Shaker Museum, Old Chatham, N. Y.; photo by Pinto Photo Service, Kinderhook, N. Y.)

141. Twelve-drawer tall chest of pine from the Second Family, New Lebanon. Stained red. It is a truly monumental piece, though in scale with the size of the room; it measures 83" high, 47½" wide, and 17⅞" deep. (Shakertown at Pleasant Hill, Inc.; photo by Lees Studio, Chatham, N. Y.)

139

140

141

142. An even taller piece than the one in Fig. 141, and from the same community. Pine, red-stained, with chestnut or butternut drawer-fronts. Both pieces were used with short stepladders to permit seeing into the cupboard and upper drawers. Dimensions: 98½" high, 41¾" wide, 25¾" deep. (Shakertown at Pleasant Hill, Inc.; photo by Lees Studio, Chatham, N. Y.)

143. Six-drawer curly-maple dresser from North Union. The feet were cut down by the Shakers and equipped with casters at a late period. The mixed woods indicate that it is not an early piece; it was probably made around 1880. Cherry top, walnut knobs, dark-stained curly-maple escutcheon; plain varnished finish. (Shaker Museum, Old Chatham, N. Y.; photo by Lees Studio, Chatham, N. Y.)

144. Chest of drawers from Pleasant Hill. Cherry, five drawers. To be observed are the short turned legs, characteristic of Kentucky, and almost certainly derived from Virginia furniture. Equally characteristic is the general feeling of bulkiness. (Shakertown at Pleasant Hill, Inc.)

145. Five-drawer chest from South Union, to be compared with Fig. 144. Cherry. The leg, as contrasted with the preceding piece, is not turned, but is a square extension of the corner post. The front skirting does not bow downward in the center, but slopes from each leg on a straight line to a center point. 48" long, 20⅜" deep, 44" high. (Shakertown at South Union, Ky.; photo by Lees Studio, Chatham, N. Y.)

142

143

144

145

146. Built-in cupboard in pine, with a yellow ochre stain, from Hancock. This furniture form, with chests of drawers and three storage cupboards (the two at the right are usually separable from the drawers and single cupboard) arranged as here, was typical of this Hancock-New Lebanon area. The piece was built flush with the wall and the drawers extended back into it; the room on the opposite side of this very thick partition had its own built-in facing into that room. Dimensions: height, 86½"; width, 66¼"; depth, 28¼". (Shaker Museum, Old Chatham, N. Y.; photo by Lees Studio, Chatham, N. Y.)

146

147. Another South Union dresser, this one with six drawers; unlike the one in Fig. 145, the legs are turned as were those from Pleasant Hill (Fig. 144). Height, 51"; width, 43"; depth, 20¼". Cherry. (Kentucky Museum, Western Kentucky University, Bowling Green; photo by Lees Studio, Chatham, N.Y.)

148. Blanket chest, New Lebanon. White ("punkin") pine, 41¼" long, 19" wide, 37½" high; diamond-shaped bone escutcheon screwed on. Originally painted green, but necessity dictated refinishing the piece; it is now natural. There is no built-in till. (Shaker Museum, Old Chatham, N. Y.)

149. Detail of the blanket chest in Fig. 148, showing the breadboard end of the lid. The quarter-round on the underside of the outer edge of the breadboard end is cut in with a molding plane, not applied as a separate piece.

150. Child's blanket chest from Enfield, Conn. Birch frame, pine top and panels. Length, 21"; width, 13¼"; height, 18". Original red paint, with traces of darker red graining on panels and lid edges. Inside till. (Shaker Museum, Old Chatham, N. Y.)

151. Interior of the chest in Fig. 150, showing the till. The lid of this is missing, although the peg-hinges still remain; one is visible.

147

148

149

150

151

152

153

152. Miniature chest of drawers, South Union, possibly for a child's use. Cherry, with four drawers and paneled sides; the corner posts are turned into short, stubby peg-legs, typical of Kentucky case furniture. Dimensions: 24¼" high, 21" long, 13¼" deep. (Shaker Museum, Auburn, Ky.; photo by Lees Studio, Chatham, N. Y.)

153. Sewing table from Enfield, Conn. Pine. Five drawers, with inset heart-shaped escutcheons, a quite unusual feature. Two drawers are found at each end, with one long, shallow one running at right angles between them. Dimensions: 50" long, 25½" wide, 28⅝" high. (Shaker Museum, Old Chatham, N. Y.; photo by Lees Studio, Chatham, N. Y.)

154. Close-up of the sewing table pictured in Fig. 153, showing the way the drawers are arranged. The knobs are replacements of the missing originals.

155. Cherry wardrobe from Pleasant Hill. Height to top of detachable cresting, 83";

width, 49⅛"; depth, 18½". Natural finish. The cresting comes off directly above the doors. Near the top on each side is a movable shelf for bonnets, made of solid cherry planks 1" thick, as is the rest of the piece. The base skirting follows very closely that of the famous pillar-and-scroll Connecticut shelf clocks which had a wide sale in the first third of the last century. The wardrobe probably dates from c. 1850. (Shaker Museum, Old Chatham, N. Y.)

156. Two-door press, or wardrobe, of walnut. Painted red over green, probably originally. From South Union, it measures 49" wide, 22⅜" deep and 73¾" high. This furniture form is an overwhelmingly Southern type; the North seemed to prefer multiple hangers and pegboards, as well as hanging pegboards in attic storage rooms. The use of small, graduated panels on case pieces is often seen in the South and West; the employment of diminishing sizes is an aesthetic subtlety which is most pleasing. (Shakertown at South Union, Ky.; photo by Lees Studio, Chatham, N. Y.)

154

155

156

157

158

159

160

157. Press from South Union, used for storage, primarily of clothing. Cherry, with one drawer. Height, 56"; width, 35½"; depth, 18½". The upper section has two shelves for further storage. The drawer edges in front are framed in a light wood; there is no inlay or veneer. (Shakertown at South Union, Ky.; photo by Lees Studio, Chatham, N. Y.)

158. Cherry press from South Union, rather similar to the foregoing. The base measures 19" deep and 17¾" high; the top is 11¾" deep and rises 36" above the base. Both top and base are 42" long. The top board of the cabinet section is held on by mortises and tenons, and measures 43½" by 12¾". The cabinet is equipped with two shelves. (Shakertown at South Union, Ky.)

159. A so-called "plantation desk" from South Union. As seems to have been customary in this area, the top is merely set on the bottom, not attached to it. The bottom section is of walnut, 39¼" long, 19½" deep and 26¼" high. The secretary top contains three shelves, and is of walnut-stained poplar, 30¼" long, 17" deep and 30¾" high. The top board has a wide overhang and measures 34¼" by 18". (Kentucky Museum, Western Kentucky University, Bowling Green; photo by Lees Studio, Chatham, N. Y.)

160. A between-doors cupboard, found in the dining room of the Center House at Pleasant Hill. Standing as it does between the two entrance doors to the room, it splays outward from the back to allow for the swing of the dining-room doors. Quite likely added after the building was erected. Height, 85", 39¾" across the front, 20" deep. This might be considered a type of built-in. (Shakertown at Pleasant Hill, Inc.; photo by Lees Studio, Chatham, N. Y.)

161. Built-in corner cupboard of cherry, supported in part by the chair rail. Quite probably installed some while after the Center House, in which it is found, was built. It is located in the dining room. It measures 27" across, and is 51" high. (Shakertown at Pleasant Hill, Inc.)

161

162

162. A very early Pleasant Hill press. Of walnut, it has storage cupboards at top and bottom, and a drop-leaf in front. Noteworthy is the extensive use of flat molding as a façade trim. Height, 79"; width, 38½"; depth at bottom, 18"; at top, 13¾". The drop-leaf is 8¾" wide. (Kentucky Museum, Western Kentucky University, Bowling Green; photo by Lees Studio, Chatham, N. Y.)

163. The press in Fig. 162, showing the dropleaf up, and the arrangement of shelves within.

164. Pie-safe from South Union, about 1830. Poplar, stained a brown cherry. The tin panels are pierced inwardly, which it is said allowed insects to enter the compartment through the slots. Height, 84"; width, 49½"; depth, 18". (Shakertown at South Union, Ky.)

165. Pie-safe from South Union, about 1840. Built of poplar, originally painted blue, with the pierced tin panels painted red. These panels, unlike those of Fig. 164, are pierced outwardly, which treatment was said to have kept marauding insects on the outside of the cabinet as those pierced inwardly did not. Height, 85"; width, 44"; depth, 20". — Trestle table with white ash trestles and walnut top. Interestingly, the planks of the top run crosswise, apparently a South Union characteristic; a drop-skirting connects the planks at their outer ends. — Simple bench with semilunar cut-out, of walnut; the connecting stretcher is very high, just under the seat. Length, 54"; width, 8½"; height, 16". (Shakertown at South Union, Ky.)

163

164

165

166. Blanket box from Pleasant Hill, ultimately by way of Dr. William Pennebaker, a Shaker elder of the West Family. Walnut, with brass escutcheons and pulls, evidently original to the piece, but definitely not of Shaker manufacture. There are original offset butterfly hinges, now broken off at the top. The lock, though not the lock-plate, is a replacement. The breadboard ends of the lid are affixed with iron pins, not wooden pegs, through a hidden dovetail. All other pegging is also of iron, said to be occa-sionally found in the Shaker West. The till is 3″ deep, with a cover which is not peg-hinged at the ends in the usual way. Dimensions: 30½″ long, 15⅛″ wide, 29″ high; the top section is 12⅝″ deep inside. The type seems distinctly to have derived from the Virginia sugar chest. The Shaker provenance of the piece seems doubtful on constructional grounds, though the line of ascription is impeccable. (St. Mark's Monastery, South Union; photo by Lees Studio, Chatham, N. Y.)

167. Interior of the box in Fig. 166. (Photo by Lees Studio, Chatham, N. Y.)

168. A non-Shaker cherry sugar chest with one drawer, from Virginia. Top section deeper than would be found in a blanket box. Note resemblance to Kentucky Shaker pieces in the shape and turning of the legs, simplicity of design, diamond-shaped inlaid bone escutcheon, and single drawer with simple wooden knobs. Width, 30¾″; depth, 19½″; height, 35″. (Kentucky Museum, Western Kentucky University, Bowling Green; photo by Lees Studio, Chatham, N. Y.)

169. Wood box from Watervliet, with detachable towel rack, here shown partly removed. Pine, brown stain. Pegs on the side are for dustpan, brush, and any other cleaning impedimenta. This type of woodbox was used near a sink, so that after caring for an adjacent stove, one could wash. Dimensions: height, 35¾″; width, 30″; depth, 12¼″. Height of towel rack, 20″. (Shaker Museum, Old Chatham, N. Y.)

170. Combination desk-cupboard and wood box from Canterbury. Pine. Overall size, 91″ high, 47½″ wide, 22″ deep. The woodbox part alone is 48½″ high. This was a work piece for use in the printing office; below the cupboard section are two pull-out slides. Beside it on the left stands the only known extant Shaker printing press, from Mt. Lebanon, used for printing herb-package labels. To its left, with the same provenance, is a low pine compositor's make-up rack, to hold temporarily the loose type set in label make-up, and which was later locked into forms. Pine, stained red. (Shaker Museum, Old Chatham, N. Y.; photo by Lees Studio, Chatham, N. Y.)

166

167

168

169

170

171

172

171. Pine secretary-chest, Mt. Lebanon. Pine, unfinished; plank doors with breadboard ends top and bottom; c. 1830. Pigeonhole "canopies" show the influence of those in slant-top desks of the period. A Palladian inspiration, they are also found not only in the triple windows of Federal houses, but in the doors of the majority of tall clock bonnets. Plank doors similar to those at the top are used at the bottom. (Private collection)

172. Glass-front secretary from Watervliet, c. 1830. Pine, natural finish. Height, 84⅝; width, 53⅝"; depth, 19". The characteristic Watervliet molding extends outward 1¾", and is 3¼" in overall height. The glass is original; the drawers and door have tin escutcheons. Originally there were but two shelves; two others have been set in but may be removed. (Private collection; photo by Lees Studio, Chatham, N. Y.)

173. Built-in chest and cupboard from Hancock, c. 1825. Pine, yellow-brown stain. Height, 90"; width, 65⅝"; depth, 20½". The closet section at the right is separable (as was usually the case) from the drawers and cupboard at the left, though always found set up as it is here; the separation was probably for ease in building and installing. Built-ins of this sort were very common, particularly in the North; this particular arrangement of drawers and cupboards seems found most commonly at Hancock and New Lebanon. With the piece built into the wall, no furniture extended out into the room; the chamber on the other side of the partition had a similar arrangement. (Shaker Museum, Old Chatham, N. Y.; photo by Louis H. Frohman, Bronxville, N. Y.)

174. Built-in closets and sets of storage drawers, attic of the Church Family Dwelling, Canterbury. Pine, perhaps as early as 1795. (Photo by Lees Studio, Chatham, N. Y.)

173

174

175

176

175. Maple bedstead, Mt. Lebanon. Can be taken completely apart by removing keys at the corner posts. Red stain. Fairly late, following the rope-bed period. Mattress supported by longitudinal slats, now missing, the slots for which can be seen under the headboard. Legs terminate in swiveling casters, characteristic of late beds of the 1880's. Early beds, if they do not have plain, simple legs, terminate in non-swiveling roller-wheels, generally set so that the piece will roll sidewise from the wall, not endwise. (Museum, Sabbathday Lake Shakers, Me.; photo by Lees Studio, Chatham, N. Y.)

176. Bed from Mt. Lebanon, mid-nineteenth century. Maple, natural finish. Used by Eldress Emma Neale. The mattress is supported by a series of cross-slats joined by inch-wide cotton tapes. Length, 71⅝"; width, 32"; height from floor, 12½". The trundle bed underneath is equipped with rollers; the mattress is supported by cross-ropes. Part of the bed-wrench used for tightening these ropes is seen at the extreme left. The frame of the trundle bed is painted a soft gray-green, and measures 64½" long, 32" wide and 6½" from the floor. (Shaker Museum, Old Chatham, N. Y.)

177. Regular bed and two trundle beds from Pleasant Hill. The large bed is painted a dark blue-green, and has the rollers (*not* casters) which allowed it to be pulled sidewise away from the wall. All three beds have rope supports for the mattress, and the usual massive Western chamfered corner posts. Cherry. (Shakertown at Pleasant Hill, Inc.; photo by Lees Studio, Chatham, N. Y.)

178. Child's folding bed. Probably pine, painted a light blue. South Union. Top part, 57" high, 31¾" wide, 6¾" deep. Overall length of bed when let down, including the standing case-headboard, 55"; depth of the mattress box, 6½". The legs automatically fold down when the bed is opened for use. When shut up (like the later patented Murphy bed), a tall-back settle is formed, with an open storage space beneath. (Shakertown at South Union, Ky.)

177

179. Bed, South Union. Cherry, of heavy stock like the majority of Western Shaker pieces. The square legs with "sausage"-turned sections are common in Kentucky; the frame is pegged. The headboard has a bolster-turned rail fixed to the top, distinctly reminiscent of the Empire style. The hoghair mattress is supported by a coil spring foundation not of Shaker manufacture, but probably contemporary with the piece. (Shakertown at South Union, Ky.; photo by Lees Studio, Chatham, N. Y.)

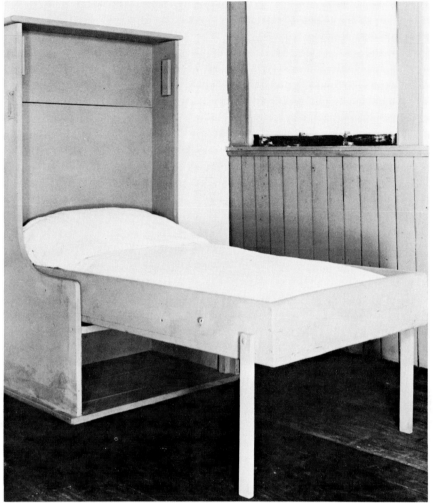

178

179

180

181

182

180. Shoemaker's bench, from the Church Family, Mt. Lebanon. While not furniture in the strict sense, it still partakes of enough of the nature of furniture to be included here. The seat back, like those of the wagon seats, folds down. The back slat is padded and leather-covered, as is the seat, which is further embellished on the edge with a scalloped leather fringe. The earliest of several dates penciled on the drawer-bottoms is 1841. The large bottom drawer is a crude later addition. Frame and drawers are of pine; legs and back are of maple. The back, which holds the drawers, is 31" high and 24¼" across the front; it is 7½" deep at the top. The overall length is 46". (Shaker Museum, Old Chatham, N. Y.; photo by Lees Studio, Chatham, N. Y.)

181. Detail of a work stool. Note that below and above the holes for the rounds, the legs have been turned down to reduce weight, but kept at the original size at the junction of the rounds for strength. Leather seat, maple frame stained red. Height, 22¾"; seat, 12" square. (Shaker Museum, Old Chatham, N. Y.)

182. While not properly a piece of furniture, this butterworker from Enfield, Conn. (used to extract buttermilk from the freshly churned butter) is included to show the fine workmanship and care put into domestic work-pieces, as well as the extraordinary use of a rare furniture wood in such a piece—tiger-stripe maple. Overall length, 43⅜"; 21¼" wide at the back, 6¼" at the front; 33¾" high at the back, 28¾" at the front, where the drain spout is located. The leg braces are, oddly, of pine; the presser-arm is of plain rock maple. (Shaker Museum, Old Chatham, N. Y.)

183. Special presentation oval box, made for Eldress Emily M. Offord of Mt. Lebanon in 1869. While not a piece of furniture, the oval box was very generally associated with furniture and was an exceedingly characteristic item. It was used as a general container (but never as a cheese box). The multiple delicate "fingers," used primarily for strength but serving also as an unobjectionable element of grace and beauty, mark such boxes as of Shaker manufacture; "World's" boxes did not employ fingers of this type. The heavily carved lid, so thoroughly mid-Victorian, is exceedingly rare, and such work was generally forbidden. Obviously, in deference to her rank, the usual prohibition was set aside for Eldress Emily. Maple sides, pine top and bottom; 5¾" long, 2½" deep. (Shaker Museum, Old Chatham, N. Y.)

184. Bottom of the box in Fig. 183, showing Eldress Emily's signature and the date. Signed and dated Shaker artifacts are rare.

184

183

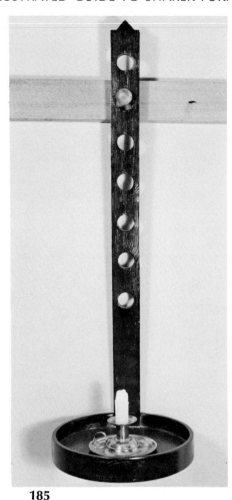

185

185. Tall candle sconce from Union Village. Very similar to those from Pleasant Hill, except that the hanger terminates at the top in a triangular gable, while those from Pleasant Hill terminate in a bow. In both types, the rim around the holder is turned into the board, and is not an applied strip. (Warren County Museum, Lebanon, Ohio; photo by Lees Studio, Chatham, N. Y.)

186. Candle sconce made for two candlesticks. From South Union. Ash, 28½" long, with a 21" shelf. Candle sconces of the Western communities are much larger than those of the North, possibly because the rooms tended to be monumental in scale. Sconces were suspended from the ubiquitous pegboards. (Shakertown at South Union, Ky.)

187. Mirror and mirror-hanger from Hancock, Maple. The hanger was shaped like a draughtsman's T-square, with a grooved transverse piece at the bottom to hold the mirror. The hanger was suspended either directly on the wall, as here, or (with a larger hole at the top) from the pegboard. Hangers often had one or more small pegs (in this example, one small brass one) at the bottom to hold small objects like combs and brushes. Hanger, 18" long, support, 12". The mirror, in a Shaker-made maple frame, is 12" by 14", a usual retiring-room (bedroom) size. Frames were usually flat, with triangular corner splines inserted; the frame was actually held together not by glue at the

corners but by a backing board tacked to the frame on all four sides. A ring at the top was connected by a string or wire to the hanger proper; by lengthening or shortening this string, the angle of the mirror could be adjusted. Note the extremely rare use of veneer on this flat-molded frame; about 1/16" thick, at least twice the normal thickness of veneer, it is of maple, and applied over pine. (Shaker Museum, Old Chatham, N. Y.)

188. Fireplace door from Union Village. Brown walnut. This unusual type of "furniture" seems unique to Union Village, and was used to shut off the fireplace after the fire had died down, thus keeping the heat in the room. (This was before the day of chimney dampers.) In this specimen, the single door is hinged at the left; double doors, hinged to either side, are occasionally found. Once in a while a single door is met with, simply set into the opening without hinges. Frequently the back of these fireplace doors is scorched or charred, showing that they were closed before the fire had sufficiently died down. Overall dimensions about 3 by 4 feet. (Warren County Museum, Lebanon, Ohio; photo by Lees Studio, Chatham, N. Y.)

189. Section of a typical pegboard. Maple, with a brownish finish. At New Lebanon and Hancock about half the pegs were threaded into the board itself; the rest are friction-driven, as are, with very rare excep-

186

187

tions, all those found at the other communities. In this illustration, one of the pegs has been backed out of the board to show the threading, done on hand-made Shaker threading machines. Note the plaster line at the bottom, near the right-hand peg. These pegboards were nailed directly to the laths, and then the wall was plastered up to the board. For this reason purists amongst collectors never remove this plaster line. Also, pegs very often extend through the board an appreciable distance; they entered into the space between the laths. Pegs average about 4″ long for normal house use. Almost every room and corridor of every Shaker building was bordered by these pegboards at a height of usually six feet. (Shaker Museum, Old Chatham, N. Y.)

190. Ceiling pegboard, probably from Hancock. A rare form, designed to be affixed to the slope of an attic roof. Length, 6′6″. (Shaker Museum, Old Chatham, N. Y.; photo by Lees Studio, Chatham, N. Y.)

191. Sill board with three pegs, installed under many window sills for holding cleaning equipment, sewing implements, etc. Pine, stained brown, with maple pegs. The board measures 41½″ long by 2½″ wide; the pegs are ¾″ long. Like the regular pegboards, these sillboards were originally attached directly to the laths, and the plaster was brought up to them. (Shaker Museum, Old Chatham, N. Y.)

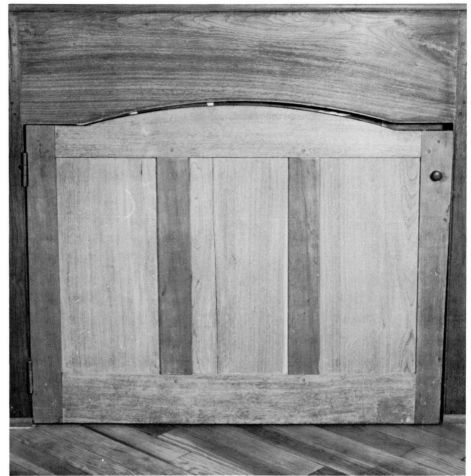

188

189

190

191

4. CLOCKS

So far as we know, all of the Shaker clockmakers came from the North, and had either been trained in their craft in Connecticut before they "believed," like Benjamin Youngs, or had been apprenticed to clockmakers. Whether these craftsmen made their own cases is a moot question; it is probable that for the most part they did not, but allowed their movements to be cased by the brethren in the cabinet shops. One brilliant exception to this was Isaac Newton Youngs, brother to Benjamin Seth and nephew to Benjamin. Since Isaac used the backboard of the cases as the back plate of his movements, he was forced to finish the rest of the case as part of the job. He and Amos Jewett made their own dials. It is probable that Benjamin Youngs, like most clockmakers of his day, bought the majority of his dials in England already made up; he either painted his name on these commercial dials, or had this done in England by the manufacturer.

Those clockmakers of whom we have definite knowledge are listed below in alphabetic order:

*Brackett, Oliver (1800–1869), Alfred
*Brackett, Reuben (1791–1867), Alfred
 Corbett, Thomas (1780–1857), Canterbury
 Jewett, Amos (1753–1834), New Lebanon
 Merrill, Granville (1839–1878), Sabbathday Lake
 Wells, Calvin (1772–1853), Watervliet
*Winkley, John (1767–1813), Canterbury
 Youngs, Benjamin (1736–1818), Watervliet
 Youngs, Benjamin Seth (1774–1855), Watervliet
 Youngs, Isaac Newton (1793–1865), New Lebanon
 Youngs, Seth, Jr. (1746–1815), New Lebanon

The Youngs family came from Hartford and Windsor, Connecticut, and were well-known clockmakers there. Seth, Sr., left his tools to his sons Joseph, Seth, Jr., and Benjamin, the last of whom was one of the founders of the Watervliet, New York, community. Benjamin usually made tall clocks,

*Left Order.

all with brass movements so far as is known. Some of the cases were of cherry, but most were of pine. Miniature tall clocks, today called "grandmother" clocks, were also an important part of his output. So, too, were "alarum" clocks, sent out to various Shaker societies around 1812. None are known to have been for sale to the World.

Benjamin Seth's clock movements were evidently few in number, and were of brass; only two or three still exist, and there seems to be no documentary evidence of any particular output. Isaac Newton Youngs, perhaps the most interesting and versatile of the trio, made only shelf or wall clocks, all with wooden movements, except of course for the verge and escape wheel. These movements were of the so-called straight-line type with the pinions set in a straight vertical line, one above the other. In addition to his horological interests, he was a stone carver—he lettered the Fountain Stone for Groveland—and was interested in music. In addition to writing a little book on musical harmony and notation, he invented a "tone-ometer," a stringed instrument for setting pitches, and a "mode-ometer," an early metronome based on the pendulum, used for setting the rhythms for the Shaker religious dances. He was also a skilled blacksmith, tinsmith, tailor, cabinetmaker, farmer, mason and spinster, doing much of the spinning of yarns used by the sisters. The clock cases made by him were of pine, varnished outside and stained a chrome yellow within. By experiment he found silver bushings for his pinion pivots to be the most satisfactory—in interesting contradiction to the work of most clockmakers, who made wooden movements with oak plates, the pivot holes in which were generally left without any bushings at all. All his recorded clocks were timepieces. (By definition, a "timepiece" merely told the time; a "clock" also struck the hours.)

Brother Thomas Corbett of Canterbury was another extraordinary genius. Not only did he make clocks for that community, but also electrostatic machines for use in the infirmary there. He was exceedingly active in the medical department, being therefore frequently spoken of as "Doctor" Corbett. He also designed and built the fire engine used at Canterbury (of the hand-tub variety), which over the years did yeoman service.

Amos Jewett, while he made many clocks, is, so far as is known, represented today by only one signed tall clock, in a private collection, and by a very early paper-covered dial, No. 12, dated 1789, in the Shaker Museum at Old Chatham.

Calvin Wells of Watervliet came of a Shaker family, famous not only for its size (there were fourteen children), but for its eminence in many fields of endeavor. None of his clocks is known to be extant, although his work is attested by many manuscript references. It is quite likely that he was apprenticed to Benjamin Youngs.

The Brackett brothers, both working c. 1825, were briefly members of the Alfred community. While there, one or the other (it has not been determined which) made the tall clock presently in the Ministry Shop of Sabbathday Lake. It is, so far as is known, the only extant example of his work. The case has been somewhat modified over the years; the dial is unsigned, and there is nothing especially remarkable about the movement, which is of brass. John Winkley, for three years a member of the Canterbury community (1792–1795), was a cousin of the more famous Shaker deacon Francis Winkley, also of Canterbury. After leaving the Shakers, John went to Durham, N. H., where he died on May 8, 1813. He is represented by only two clocks currently known, both with exquisitely engraved brass dials: one, in the Henry Ford Museum at Dearborn, is a very choice case-on-case shelf clock with a kidney-shaped opening in the door; the other is a coffin-shaped shelf clock in a private collection in Cornish, N. H.; the case has been badly butchered over the years. Both clocks have brass movements.

One of the latest of the Shaker clockmakers was Elder Granville Merrill of Sabbathday Lake. It is quite probable that he was not a clockmaker in the sense or to the extent that the others cited were, but he was a mechanic of so high a degree of excellence as to be accounted by his peers a near genius. Apparently no mechanical problem was too complicated for him to solve. He fabricated many clever machines for use in the cabinet shops; he designed and built a small steam engine used in the Sisters' Shop to drive machinery used in some of their minor industries. And he made a "tower clock" for use in the community. This was very different from any of the other clocks we have heretofore mentioned.

It consisted of an old tall clock movement with an engraved brass dial, almost certainly English. To the strike train Elder Granville attached tripping levers that activated a heavy count wheel and ancillary mechanisms powered by a hundred-pound weight that dropped sixty feet from the attic to the basement of the Brethren's Shop. This large iron count wheel, when activated by the old clock movement, struck the hours on an eighty-pound brass engine bell mounted on the outside wall of the shop. There was never an outside dial; the clock was designed merely to strike the hours. This ingenious device has been installed at the Shaker Museum in Old Chatham. It is not known that Elder Granville made any other horological machinery. His painful and untimely death at the age of 39 from erysipelas was sincerely mourned. The heir to his mechanical ability was Elder Delmer C. Wilson (1873–1961), last of the Shaker brethren. Apparently Elder Delmer never did anything with clocks but repair them.

As a sort of footnote to the clockmaker's trade we may note the making of sundials. There are currently only two known to exist: one begun by Benjamin S. Youngs, finished and erected by Elder Harvey L. Eads in 1867, and now mounted at the Shaker Museum in Old Chatham; the other, decidedly cruder, now in the Smithsonian Institution in Washington. It was made by an anonymous craftsman in 1836 at Mt. Lebanon. Ancillary information seems to indicate that it might well have been the work of Isaac N. Youngs, who, as has been noted, was of an experimenting turn of mind, and was never far removed from the measuring of time in various fields. Undoubtedly other sundials were made, but we have no present record of them.

192. Wall clock by Benjamin Youngs, Watervliet. Pine coffin-case, stained red. "Alarum" model (note the inner dial). Wall or shelf clocks by Benjamin Youngs are exceedingly rare, as he generally made tall ("grandfather") clocks. Also unusual is the one-word spelling of "Watervliet," which he generally divided into two words. Dimensions: 41½" high, 10" wide at the base, 9½" at the top; 5½" deep. (Western Reserve Historical Society Museum, Cleveland; photo by Elroy Sanford, Willoughby Hills, Ohio)

193. Tall clock by Benjamin Youngs, Watervliet. Movement of brass, made between 1790 and 1805; signed English dial; pine case by Erastus Rude of New Lebanon, 1811. Height, 85¼". (Shaker Museum, Old Chatham, N. Y.; photo by Lees Studio, Chatham, N. Y.)

194. Two shelf clocks. Left: alarm clock with upside-down movement (note position of the winding holes) by B[enjamin] S[eth] Youngs of Watervliet. The brass dial around the post for the hands is the alarm setting-dial; the seconds-dial is at the top. Pine case. About 1820. Apparently Benjamin S. Youngs, nephew to Benjamin Youngs, made very few clocks, though he was trained as a clockmaker. Right: timepiece, with neither alarm nor strike, by B[enjamin] Youngs, uncle of the preceding; Watervliet, c. 1810. Cherry case of the coffin type. (Henry Ford Museum, Dearborn, Mich.; photo by Elmer R. Pearson, Chicago)

195. Wag-on-the-wall clock by Isaac Newton Youngs, brother to Benjamin Seth Youngs. An Arabic "1" on the back plate suggests that this might be Isaac's first clock, made for the Elders' Shop in 1815. The dustboard covering the top of the movement shows that the timepiece was never intended to be cased. Wooden works and dial; hands cut and filed manually. A staple in the backboard was for hanging

192

193

194

195

over a nail. The dial is 10″ square, pine, with painted rings and chapters; unsigned. The clock is wound by pulling the cord, which is wound about the barrel of the first wheel, the other end being attached to the heavy weight. Bone click and click-spring. (Hancock Shaker Community, Inc.)

196. Wall or shelf clock by Isaac N. Youngs, Mt. Lebanon, made there and dated 1840. Pine case, 31″ high, 10″ wide, 3″ deep; door is set with two lights of glass; finish is a red stain outside, chrome yellow inside. The movement is of the "straight-line" type, and is numbered 21 on the back of the dial. The backboard, which doubles as the

back plate of the movement, is extended at the top to a cresting, drilled through to allow the clock to be hung from a pegboard. The 30-hour movement is weight-driven and does not strike—a "timepiece." (Hancock Shaker Community, Inc.; photo by Elmer R. Pearson, Chicago)

197. Detail of construction of an Isaac N. Youngs cased wall timepiece. The walnut backboard of the case is simultaneously the back plate of the movement; the pillars supporting the front plate are set directly into it. Youngs evidently thought he had devised this arrangement, although some non-Shaker Connecticut clockmakers also

made use of it. Although he came of a famous clockmaking family, Youngs says he was apprenticed to Amos Jewett of Mt. Lebanon. Dimensions of this backboard-plate are 31″ long by 10″ wide. The pivots for the five-wheel train were set into short brass strips placed across holes drilled into the backboard; these holes were necessary to accommodate the protruding ends of the pivots. The pendulum was hung from the slotted wooden stud situated between the two top pillars. In some of Isaac's earliest movements these bushing strips were of steel; as these quickly cut the pivots, he substituted silver or brass. (Hancock Shaker Community, Inc.)

198. Clock stand from the South Union Trustee's Office. (The clock is not Shaker-made.) Pine, stained yellow, 77″ high, 17″ wide, 7½″ deep. Clocks in the North were generally either hung from the pegboards or supported on shelves attached to the wall. In this Western example, storage space is provided underneath, and small hanging-pegs are inserted into the outer sides. (Shaker Museum, Auburn, Ky.; photo by Lees Studio, Chatham, N. Y.)

196

197

198

5. STOVES

Cast-iron stoves, properly speaking, are not furniture, but are here included because they were so intimately and necessarily associated with furniture, and were so typically Shaker in design—and are also so collectable today. The oldest such stoves were evidently derived from the so-called "Franklin stove" —though not the type that Ben Franklin himself invented. Quite early the Shakers decided that to put the door and ash-shelf at the end rather than on the long side would be more efficient, and all subsequent Shaker stoves were of this type, with a number of interesting variations often found.

Intended only for burning wood, they were not equipped with grates. The fire was built directly on the bed plate, which had to be protected against heat-cracking by a layer of ash or of sand. These stoves were used only for heating; for cooking, big wood-burning ranges were built of brick with cast-iron tops. Ovens were separate from ranges, though erected near them in the kitchens. (One at Canterbury has a set of revolving iron shelves for baking pots of beans and other goodies.) These were most often of the inside beehive type, and made use of a peel obligatory.

The stoves came in many different sizes and with some variation of form, as will be seen in the accompanying illustrations. One was the super-heater, a smaller stove set above the main stove, with two peg-legs in front, and with the back supported by the smoke hole of the main stove beneath. In such an arrangement the stovepipe rose from the front of the super-heater. Thus the heat went from the lower to the upper stove and thence up the stovepipe to the chimney. What many do not today realize is that with care in damper control the stovepipe itself radiated a good deal of heat, thus helping to warm the room.

Most communities had small foundries in which stoves and smallish castings were made. A few, notably Sabbathday Lake and, in later days, Canterbury, in the North, and the Kentucky communities in the West, apparently never made their own castings, but constructed the wooden patterns for them and sent them out to commercial foundries.

A later and more efficient, though less attractive, form developed at Canterbury. In this model the body of the stove comprised five parts—the four sides and the top—all held together with stove bolts. The top, in turn, consisted of two parts hinged together; the back portion, with the smoke hole, was fastened to the bed plate by long bolts, but the front formed a liftable lid, thus making it easier to feed wood into the stove. The sides were like panels—unlike the old "canonical" stoves, the tops of which, except for the doors, were cast in one piece and held to the bed plate by weight alone.

The stoves made in the West, though of the usual Shaker pattern (Canterbury alone made the paneled type), were notably heavier and more massive in design though of comparable size. Indeed, many look even crude, particularly those made for South Union.

A rare and interesting variety of stove found at Watervliet was the sheet-iron model. This was cylindrical; one in the Shaker Museum in Old Chatham has a cast-iron hearth and door, two cast-iron legs in front and one in back cast integral with the back plate. Another, in the Ford Museum in Dearborn, is entirely of sheet iron, and is also a tripod model. Like the non-Shaker "airtight" stove of fifty years ago (a type still, by the way, being made), this heated up very rapidly but, of course, lost heat with equal rapidity once the fire was allowed to go down. It was also much shorter-lived than a cast-iron stove. We do not know why these were made or used, but one is permitted to guess that they were a form used in shops, designed to take the chill quickly off a room until possibly a larger cast-iron stove could warm up and take over.

Ironing stoves were another distinct variety, used only in the wash shops. These were, of course, of cast iron, usually of the typical design, but with a slight difference—a ledge was cast along each side, which sloped more sharply than was usual. The heels of the sadirons were set on this ridge and the soles rested on the stove sides. Some heating stoves were adapted to the purpose by riveting strap-iron shelves to the sides. Two or three very large ones are known, built in the general form of the old-fashioned potbelly stoves, but with polygonal, not round, sides; strap-iron shelves were ranged around the body in several tiers, and over the whole a sheet-iron cover was placed, with trap doors at spaced intervals to give access to the sadirons ranged on the shelves within.

It is interesting to note that from earliest times, with two or three exceptions, all Northern Shaker buildings were designed for stoves; the chimneys were small, as contrasted with those of Western communities, where heating was very generally done by fireplaces until quite late. At Union Village there appears a "furniture" form associated with this type of heating that seems unique. In that community a great many fireplaces were either catercorner (as also in Kentucky) or set flush with the wall but close to a corner; to close them off at night when the fire had gone down, and thus conserve the heat in the room, paneled wooden doors were constructed. Sometimes these were merely set into the fireplace embrasure; more often, they were hinged at one side and were swung to like a gate. Occasionally, double fireplace doors were used, divided in the middle, and swung out from both sides. We often find these charred on the inside from having been closed too soon, before the fire had died down sufficiently. In no buildings that the author has seen were there mantelpieces or mantel shelves except in the kitchens, and there only consisting of a simple plank shelf. The often elaborate side paneling so frequently found in early homes contemporary with the Shakers is entirely or almost entirely missing; at best, a single-brick facing is used.

199

200

199. Early stove, Canterbury, c. 1795. Tripod base (third leg hidden at the back). Lift-lid adjustable by the attached wrought-iron arm to various sizes of opening; it can also be wedged shut. Said to be the earliest Shaker stove extant. Design based on the so-called "Franklin stove," though not on that invented by Dr. Franklin himself. (Shaker Museum, Old Chatham, N. Y.; photo by Lees Studio, Chatham, N. Y.)

200. Stove, perhaps from Hancock. The base is cast in strap form. The small draft door is missing. The heavy chamfer around the top is unusual. (Shaker Museum, Old Chatham, N. Y.; photo by Elmer R. Pearson, Chicago)

201. Stove designed and made at New Lebanon. The legs and stretchers are of wrought iron, with "penny" feet; the mortising in of the stretchers is a rare feature. Hinged draft door. The top has an opening hinged to the solid top of the stove, for the insertion of small pieces of wood. This is an uncommon design. (Shaker Museum, Old Chatham, N. Y.; photo by Elmer R. Pearson, Chicago)

202. Meetinghouse stove, one of four used to heat the great meetinghouse at New Lebanon. Of the same design as the usual "Hancock" type, it is much larger; the top measures 32½" long by 15½" wide, and stands 24½" from the floor. The ash-shelf extends out 12". The draft regulator differs from those on other stoves of this type in that it is a piece of heavy strap iron 1⅛" wide and 12⅛" long (the entire width of the door); a handle attached to it extends back and is designed to fit against the inner edge of the lip of the ash-shelf to lock the draft-bar in place. (Shaker Museum, Old Chatham, N. Y.; photo by Elmer R. Pearson, Chicago)

201

202

203

204

203. New Lebanon stove, of the double-decker type, used for extra radiation. Upper section is removable. Height to the top of the main section, 16½"; of the upper section, including legs, 6½". Length, including ash-hearth, 28¾"; width, 10¾". There are no grates in Shaker heating stoves; the fire was built on the bed plate, which was protected from direct contact with the heat by a layer of sand or ash. (Shaker Museum, Old Chatham, N. Y.; photo by Lees Studio, Chatham, N. Y.)

204. Improved stove of the Canterbury type. This late model (c. 1870) was not cast by the Shaker foundrymen; while the patterns were made in the Shaker shops, the stoves are said to have been cast at the Ford Foundry of Concord, N. H. The paneled sides are held to each other by stove bolts, and the top is attached to the sides by long bolts passing through both top and bottom. The top has a hinged front section that will lift up to facilitate the putting in of wood; The draft is regulated by a slide on the ash-hearth in front. This slide can be lifted entirely out to make easier the removal of ash from the little well cast in the bed of the hearth, or slid forward to reduce or cut off the draft flowing under the door. (Shaker Museum, Old Chatham, N. Y.; photo by Elmer R. Pearson, Chicago)

205. Laundry stove from New Lebanon. A strap-iron shelf is welded to each side to hold the irons to be heated. This stove was adapted from the super-heater model (Fig. 203), as can be told by the rectangular smoke hole which was designed to connect with the back of the super-heater. The original wooden knob on the latch long ago charred off from the heat. (Shaker Museum, Old Chatham, N. Y.; photo by Elmer R. Pearson, Chicago)

206. Laundry stove from the South Family shops, New Lebanon, and probably cast there. The sides have a more pronounced incline than usual to accommodate the sadirons, the heels of which were supported by the ridge cast integral with the side. The purpose of the depressed top has not been clearly ascertained, but was probably so made to keep the irons set thereon from overheating. The wooden knob of the latch has charred off, and the small draft door has been lost. (Shaker Museum, Old Chatham, N. Y.; photo by Elmer R. Pearson, Chicago)

205

206

207

207. Stove from South Union, of the superheater variety. Noteworthy is the clumsiness of the proportions, although they follow the Northern pattern. The left leg of the superheater is a Shaker replacement of a broken original. The draft slide has long been lost. (St. Mark's Monastery, South Union, Ky.; photo by Elmer R. Pearson, Chicago)

208. Stove from Pleasant Hill, with superheater and tripod base. The delicacy of treatment is not generally characteristic of Kentucky stoves; it may well be a Northern piece imported into Pleasant Hill as a pattern for those to be made there. It is said that Pleasant Hill stoves were never cast in a community foundry, but were manufactured from Shaker-made patterns in a commercial foundry. (Shaker Museum, Old Chatham, N. Y,; photo by Elmer R. Pearson, Chicago)

209. Sheet-iron stove from Watervliet. This is a very rare form, as most stoves were cast. This example has a cast-iron front and back section, to which the legs are attached; only the body is sheet-iron. The Shaker-made "elbow" for the attachment of the stovepipe to the stove is interesting and ingenious. (Shaker Museum, Old Chatham, N. Y.; photo by Elmer R. Pearson, Chicago)

210. Sheet-iron stove from Watervliet or New Lebanon. A very rare type, it differs from the preceding in that the entire stove, with the exception of the three legs, is of sheet metal. (The stove in the background is not Shaker.) (Henry Ford Museum, Dearborn, Mich.; photo by Elmer R. Pearson, Chicago)

208

209

210

6. DECADENT AND DOUBTFUL PIECES

During the past few years an increasing, though mercifully small, number of pieces, usually chairs, have been brought to the author for identification and authentication, and which are Shaker by inspiration, derivation or very late genuine construction. This particular aspect of his duties is not, frankly, his happiest. The proud owner of an artifact is sure his prize is Shaker, and is not overwhelmed with joy to learn either that it is not, or, if genuine, represents Shaker design at its worst. Illustrations of a few of these pieces are here included.

The classical period of Shaker furniture may be dated from 1790 to 1840; many feel that the finest pieces were produced at Hancock and New Lebanon, although most of the New England communities were not very far behind. The design of Shaker pieces found in the Western communities never measured up to the standard of the Northern furniture, with a few brilliant exceptions. These observations do not, however, entitle one to aesthetic snobbery; one of the most exquisitely proportioned pieces in the collections of the Shaker Museum at Old Chatham, N. Y., is a Mt. Lebanon child's high chair made in 1880; a Canterbury butternut dining table of the same period runs it a close second.

As has been noted before, once a Shaker craftsman had evolved a design that was both useful and pleasing, he saw no reason whatever for changing it. Country folk are conservative by nature, and religious communities doubly so. When change did occur, as was bound to happen, it came slowly.

It is a bit of a shock, therefore, to many collectors, especially beginning collectors, and to those brought up on the standard books on Shaker furniture, to discover that the overpowering influence of the Victorian styles invaded Shakerdom. Not every Shaker piece is by any means a stylistic masterwork. Many examples from the late period are downright ugly, although the workmanship is still superb.

To their eternal credit be it recorded that the Shakers resisted the horrors of Victorianism longer than almost any other segment of the American public, and when at length they did succumb, their inherited conservatism and the remnants of Mother Ann's strictures on design prevented their falling into the worst abysses.

An example in point is the bentwood rocker, which, along with the spindle-back, never appeared in any of the chair catalogues. This design was not, evidently, made for the Philadelphia Centennial Exposition of 1876 (where the Believers had a booth), as was once thought. Indeed, its origins are very obscure. Recently such a chair turned up bearing a label identifying it as made by the Henry I. Seymour Chair Manufactory of West Troy [Watervliet], N. Y., and bearing patent dates of Sept. 9, 1873, and Feb. 23, 1875. Research has revealed that these patents were both taken out in the names of Grove B. Harwood of Troy, and Robert Wood of West Troy, and were numbered successively 6875 and 8163 in the "chair design" category. The first patent was primarily for a taped back and seat, and secondarily for an armless rocker with a cushion rail using this taping; the second patent was for a bentwood chair like those associated with the Shakers (Fig. 214), with a taped back and seat. So far no assignment of patent rights to Henry I. Seymour has been found.

In the rolls of the Watervliet Shaker community there is found a large family of Harwoods, and a smaller one of Woods; although no connection has so far been found between the Shakers and the patentees of the same name, one is tempted to think that either Harwood or Wood might briefly have been Shakers and left, or else were related to Shakers. After all, Troy or West Troy were only some thirty-five miles from Mt. Lebanon and six or seven from the Watervliet Shakers, and visiting amongst the communities and their friends was constant. It is entirely conceivable that the patentees appropriated designs worked out or produced by the Believers (and which would have been unprotected), and patented them as their own, then engaged Seymour to manufacture the chairs. Seymour might also have been a silent partner. Some credence is lent to this theory by the fact that, long before Patent #6875 was granted for taping backs and seats, the Shakers had universally used seating tapes, and in the checkerboard design later patented.

Did only the Henry I. Seymour Chair Manufactory (1852-1885) make bentwoods, or did the Shakers also? Such little evidence as is presently at hand is ambivalent. When the Hancock Community ceased to function in 1960, one private collector bought a fairly large supply of unassembled bentwood chair parts, which probably came over from Mt. Lebanon with other materials when that community closed. It is highly unlikely that the Shakers would either have assembled Seymour chairs or have bought out Seymour stocks. At the present time the story of both bentwoods and spindle-backs is extremely muddy and confusing, and no incontrovertible evidence has come to light to clarify the situation.

The Shaker bentwood, whatever its origin, was a far cry from Thonet's. Only the back and arms were bent; the back posts swept up to form the back, and the front posts continued as arms. There were none of the dust-catching curlycues that characterized the Viennese types and their American imitations. The lines were clean and uncluttered, as befitted Shaker creations.

The spindle-backs, while far removed from the canonical slat-backs that had marked Shaker chairs for a century, were also simple and dignified and were ultimately derived from the ever-popular Windsor chair (Fig. 216). Even less is known of their ancestry or designer, as no label has ever been found on any one. They were often called, for no ascertainable reason, "Brother Gregorys." Research has failed entirely to identify a putative Bro. Gregory Hawkins, said to have designed or made this style at Mt. Lebanon, or to connect any Bro. Gregory with the chair industry.

Apparently introduced around 1870, the spindle-back was made at least as late as 1929, as is proved by its appearance in a photograph so dated of the Mt. Lebanon chair sales room (Fig. 41). It is found in several sizes, both with and without arms. Armchair and straight-chair types are very rare. None is ever found with either an identifying decal or cushion rail. The finish seems to be exclusively in logwood red, varnished. The finials are more elongated than the usual Mt. Lebanon acorn finial, and with a shorter neck. It is known that this form, like the more usual designs, was copied by commercial manufacturers.

One of the abiding mysteries is why, if the Shakers made bentwood and spindle-backs, none ever appeared in any chair catalogue, despite the fact that they are by no means rare, and tend to be found in largest numbers in the Albany-Troy-New Lebanon area. Perhaps the only tenable explanation is that both forms were distinctly more difficult to make than the common ladder-back, and so represented a profit margin low enough to make it unfeasible to advertise them for wide public distribution.

The mystery is deepened by the fact that in no diary or journal, to the writer's knowledge, is any mention made of either chair type, yet one would reasonably expect such radical and distinctive designs as these, which represented so sharp a departure from the accepted norms, to have been mentioned.

The simplicity and dignity inherent in the bentwood and spindle-back chairs were not, unhappily, found in many case pieces. This was true in Maine and at Canterbury, and especially so at Enfield, Connecticut, where a Scottish convert-cabinetmaker insisted on producing pieces scarcely to be distinguished from the work of Grand Rapids of the time, to the horror of many older Believers. An example of his work is a "commode," with yellow-grained finish and carved oak-leaf walnut pulls.

In the 1890's or early 1900's apparently someone at Mt. Lebanon began producing chairs of the spindle-back variety that were perfect Gorgons. Posts were not only massive but elaborately turned, as were the spindles. Cushion rails were heavy and resembled portière rods. No shred of grace or beauty invested them. The best that can be said for them is that they are sturdy!

It is possible that these were produced by commercial manufacturers in the taste of the times, and were inspired by or imitative of Shaker chairs. At the present time there is no evidence for or against this possibility except one fact: they are seated with Shaker tape. Sister Sadie Neale is said to have refused to put this tape into chairs not made by Believers; if her feeling was correctly reported and commonly held, these pieces must have been made at the community and not in a commercial factory. Perhaps it is well that the maker is anonymous!

The author has seen one spindle-back that the owner was sure was Shaker, but which could not possibly have been. Not only did cross-stretchers connect the posts inside, but every inch of the whole chair except for the runners was wrapped in rattan, including even the finials and mushrooms. To top it off, the whole piece was enameled white.

Bentwoods are occasionally seen with routed designs on the front of the back and arm posts, picked out in gold paint on a black-enameled background.

The Shaker Empire dining chairs from Mt. Lebanon have already been mentioned. They are reasonably simple and graceful, and are the least obnoxious examples of this Victorianizing trend.

It is of interest to note that this overpowering influence seems to have left the Western communities relatively unscathed. Perhaps the reason for this is that they did far less selling to the public than did the North, primarily Mt. Lebanon; second, that commercial furniture factories supplied the desires of the public for Victorian furniture; third, Western pieces appear not to have had the same appeal to local folk that they seem to have had in the North, where the Shaker reputation for fine, sturdy and useful pieces was well established.

Lastly, when the Shaker ability to resist change sagged to the point where desire overrode tradition, there was a plethora of relatively inexpensive furniture easily obtainable. Why, with a reduced roster of cabinetmakers, should a community build these complicated pieces when they could be bought more cheaply from a dealer should the need for new pieces arise?

Shaker homes by then had changed. Buildings built or remodeled in the late 1870's or early 1880's generally lacked pegboards; linoleum and "art squares" covered the floors; platform rockers made their appearance; pianos and parlor organs, once frowned upon, were installed. The glories of Shaker simplicity and the beauty of uncluttered design were over. To preserve what has been and to inspire people of later days is the reason for the increasing number of museums and galleries today dedicated to the Order, and helps explain the current interest in things Shaker.

There are other reasons, too, for the present-day fascination with Shaker furniture. We live in a world of machine-produced perfection, inspired on the drawing board and transferred to the machine shop or furniture factory for embodiment. The craftsman's personal touch has gone. Impersonalized manufacture is not inspiring. People crave handmade things, and for this reason. Who would not prefer a unique, handcrafted setting for a fine jewel, or a piece of hand-tooled leather? In some mysterious way the craftsman's personality, his very touch and presence, if you will, shines through his work; commercial products seem to smell of the drafting board, the electric motor and machine oil. Hand-wrought iron has the charm of irregularity, of loving attention to detail totally missing in the stamped-out imitations available in hardware stores, attractive though these things may be.

In revolt against the mechanized perfectionism of our day people are increasingly visiting museums where the handmade products of an earlier day may be seen, savored and appreciated . . . and envied! Note the increasing number of small shops turning out excellent reproductions of these early pieces, and of other shops making original furniture, some of which will be classics in their own right in time to come.

Also, we live in a day of hectic rushing about, of crushing problems both personal and cosmic. Shaker furniture was produced by people who were very sure of themselves and of the faith which animated them; they lived in a world closely tied to nature and the good earth, "far from the madding crowd." As we look at these lovely pieces we invariably reflect back upon the times that produced them, and the serene folk who created them. The Utopia of which the Shakers dreamed seems to us of today to have been achieved and to have receded into the mists of the past; in our desire to possess such artifacts or fine reproductions of them we are, possibly unconsciously, trying to recapture the simplicity, beauty and peace of that bygone time, to create for ourselves, so to speak, an island fortress against the onslaughts of a world that has become too much for us to cope with. This is indeed one of the distinct contributions which the quiet Believers have left us.

211

212

213

211. Mt. Lebanon "chapel chair," made at the South Family specifically for the Meetinghouse, where such chairs were used attached in groups of four by spacer-bars under the seats at front and back. First used on Sunday, 21 August, 1887. All bear the number 3, thus refuting the legend that numbered models were made only for public sale, and only unnumbered ones for domestic use. The punched-plywood seats were very probably supplied by Gardner & Co. of New York, who had a large exhibition at the Philadelphia Centennial Exposition of 1876. This company also made benches for railroad station waiting rooms. (Shaker Museum, Old Chatham, N. Y.)

212. Detail of the "chapel chair" in Fig. 211, showing square seat rails made to accommodate the commercial punched-plywood seat. These rails could never be used for any other type of Shaker seating.

213. The number "3" stamped on the back of the top slat of the "chapel chair" in Fig. 211, which was never intended for commercial sale.

214. Bentwood rocker, ascribed to the South Family, Mt. Lebanon. An uncommon, though by no means rare, type, it seems to have been produced after 1875. It is taped in light blue and beige, and found only in a natural finish. This type of chair is found in no chair catalogue. (Private collection)

215. Bentwood rocker, with tapes removed, showing framing. Painted ebony black, with line-carved decoration on legs and back, picked out with gilt paint. A very late version of this style, quite possibly a commercial imitation, as indicated by the color. (Private collection)

216. Spindle-back rocker. This type, also never found in catalogues, came in several sizes, both with and without arms, but armchair and straight-chair types are unknown, or at least, are extremely rare. Finished only in logwood red and varnished. Made at the South Family, Mt. Lebanon, after 1875, as was the small, plank-topped maple footstool. Such footstools, if they have a decal, have it on the underside of the top, which was often fitted with a shag cushion. Like most of the regular chairs, this footstool was finished in "white" (natural, as here), logwood red or ebony black. (Shaker Museum, Old Chatham, N. Y.; photo by Lees Studio, Chatham, N. Y.)

214

215

216

217

218

217. Spindle-back rocker of very late, degenerate form, possibly Shaker-made. The wood is ash or hickory. The gallery with short, turned spindles is occasionally seen in several variations. This gallery, and the choice of wood, together with a marked heaviness and coarseness of proportion, mark this chair as of the 1910–1915 period, probably. (Private collection)

218. Another variant of the spindle-back, here seen with only five, widely spaced arrow-tipped spindles instead of the usual eight dowels. Note that the legs are not split to receive the runners, but are instead doweled into much thicker rockers. It seems probable that this is not Shaker-made, but rather was produced by some commercial firm copying, or inspired by, a Shaker original. (Private collection)

219. Mt. Lebanon rope-twisted spindle-back rocker, c. 1890–1900. Maple, with mahogany stain and replaced tape seat. One of two currently known. Typical of late Mt. Lebanon products, it is clearly influenced by contemporary taste, yet still shows Shaker restraint. Like all spindle-backs, it lacks decal and model number identification. Note the direction of the twists—outward in front, inward on the back posts. (Private collection)

220. Side view of the chair in Fig. 219. Observe the back posts, with backward curve steamed in after carving. The chord visible to the right of the post is the line of the spindles, which are straight and set into the top and bottom rounds. These are curved to fit the back, and are also visible in the photograph.

221. Detail of the back post of the chair in Fig. 219, showing the workman's scribe mark at the beginning of the rope-twist. Non-Shaker cabinetmakers would normally omit this, having marked the beginning point on the tool-rest, not on the post.

222. Detail of the finial of the chair shown in Fig. 219, turned on the end of the post, not separately made and then affixed, as might have been suspected. The finial is as atypical as the rope-turning. Note the topmost decorative scribe mark which, by the workman's error, overlaps instead of being continuous.

219

220

221

222

223

224

225

226

223. Extremely degenerate form of rocker, with original blue and beige tape. Mt. Lebanon. (Note the round runners, like those on the bentwoods.) Dowel arms and the excessively coarse bamboo turnings and gross proportions and details mark this as very late. A few chairs of this type are known, but whether they were made as a wild and unsuccessful bid for a new model to catch contemporary Edwardian taste is not known. Mahogany-finished maple. Fortunately the maker is anonymous. Interesting is the method of affixing the cushion rail. The topmost knobs are inserted into the upper half of the holes drilled through the cushion rail, the lower half being occupied by the tapered ends of the posts. (Private collection)

224. Side chair to match the rocker shown in Fig. 223. It has lost its cushion rail, which rather improves its appearance! (Private collection)

225. Unusual Mt. Lebanon rocker, apparently very rare. The back is made of plywood, curved to conform to body contours and originally padded with curled hair, remnants of which may still be seen at the lower right-hand corner. This was then covered with coarsely tooled russet leather held in place by brass-topped upholstery nails, still in place. The back posts were slotted to receive this back board, which means that the present back was not a later substitute for original slats. Two wide straps circled the posts at top and bottom, as indicated by the brighter varnish beneath them; their purpose is unknown. (Private collection)

226. Back view of the rocker in Fig. 225. Stained mahogany like the rest of the chair, this reverse side was never leather-covered as was the front.

227. Side chair from Mt. Lebanon, c. 1890, stamped and decaled #3. Noteworthy are the very unusual and atypical finials, of which only three or four examples are known. Probably an experimental model which was not continued. (Shaker Museum, Old Chatham, N. Y.)

228. Detail of the finial of the chair shown in Fig. 227.

227

228

229

230

229. Shaker dining chair in the American Empire tradition. From the Mt. Lebanon Community, with authenticity attested by the late Sr. Sadie Neale. Maple, with bent rabbit-ear posts and Empire tiger-maple slats; natural finish. The slab seat has a thin padding of curled hair under the Kelly-green figured velvet, contemporary with the chair. Probably c. 1890, a period which seems to have spawned a considerable variety of exotic models. Craftsman unknown. One of a set of a dozen or more, now scattered among several owners. (Private collection)

230. Underside of the chair in Fig. 229, showing construction of the seat and method of attachment. The slab seat could, if desired, be removed, and tapes installed over the sound rounds. On this particular example the seat is screwed to the rounds.

231. Mt. Lebanon "dining chairs," probably made for the carriage trade as boudoir chairs. The seat of the one at the left is woven in a unique diamond pattern, and is 16½" high; the chair is finished in an ebony black. The one at the right is 17½" high, and has two dowels instead of slats at the back; the finish is a brown maple stain, varnished. Late nineteenth or early twentieth century. Said to have been designed by William Perkins of the South Family, New Lebanon. (Shaker Museum, Old Chatham, N. Y.)

232. In this plate we see illustrated the confusion possible between a real dining chair and a cut-down straight chair. The piece at the left is a regular three-slat straight chair, with the finials and top slat sawed off; provenance unknown but probably New Lebanon. The one at the right is a Watervliet two-slat dining chair, made as such. Superficially both can be taken as dining chairs, and cut-down chairs are often bought or sold as such. The spacing of the slats is a completely identifying point. Chairs were frequently cut down at the back for use in shop and kitchen, but never for the dining room. Height of the back of the cut-down chair, 30½", with a half-inch taken off the bottom to remove the tilter-sockets; the height of the back of the dining chair, 25½". (Shaker Museum, Old Chatham, N. Y.)

231

232

233

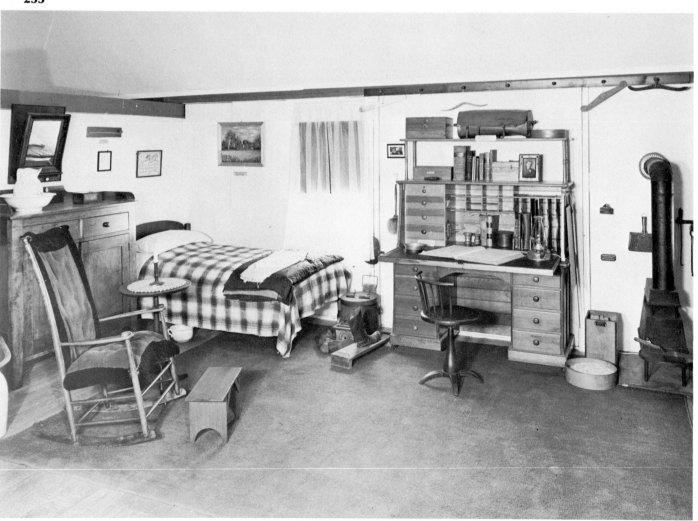

234

233. Three chairs from Canterbury, c. 1820, illustrating the technique of adapting to different uses by cutting down the legs. The one at the left, equipped with tilters, has a seat 15″ from the floor; note the height of the bottom stretchers. The two chairs to the right were originally built as a pair, in curly maple; that at the extreme right was made as a rocker, while the center one was initially a straight chair equipped with tilters like that at the left, but then cut down for a low rocker. (Note the plugged thong-holes on the inside of the back legs.) This adaptation is made obvious by the height of the seat (13½″) and by the extreme closeness of the runners to the bottom rounds; the legs have been cut down 1½″, as can be seen by comparison with the chairs to the right and left, whose seats are 15″ from the floor. The absence of any sort of taper

generally betrays a cut-down leg, especially when coupled with an unusually low bottom stretcher. (Shaker Museum, Old Chatham, N. Y.)

234. The commode at the left is from Pleasant Hill, and is of cherry. Large storage cupboards at the bottom, two drawers above; gallery around top. Dimensions: 42″ wide, 19¾″ deep, 43¾″ high without gallery. At the right is a late Elder's desk from Alfred, Me. Natural-finished pine, with a back of chestnut; drop-lid covered with black oilcloth. Made by Bro. Frank Libby in 1896. This piece shows the degeneration of Shaker design as the furniture enters the twentieth century. Dimensions: 49½″ wide, 22¼″ deep, 30″ high to the writing surface of the lid, which is 45¾″ by 18¾″ when open. To the top of the storage section it is

20¾″; the book rack crowning the whole is 12¾″ high and 12″ deep. (Shaker Museum, Old Chatham, N. Y.; photo by Louis H. Frohman, Bronxville, N. Y.)

235. Very late desk from Alfred, now in the Dwellinghouse at Sabbathday Lake. Of butternut and maple, the drawers and drop-lid are about the only parts of the piece identifiably Shaker, although the attribution is impeccable. This piece illustrates well the invidious and overpowering influence of the Victorian styles. The chair was made probably sixty years earlier. Note also the built-ins in the background, constructed when the building was built in 1883; the wooden latch-plate was to keep the door clean of finger marks. (Photo by Lees Studio, Chatham, N. Y.)

235

APPENDIX:
A SHAKER CHAIR CATALOGUE

The first Mt. Lebanon chair catalogue was issued by Elder Robert M. Wagan in 1874, apparently, although the author has never seen one dated; the first bearing a date seems to be one issued in Canaan, N. Y., in 1875, followed by that of 1876, printed for the Philadelphia Centennial Exposition. This last was more elaborate than any other, containing as it did line cuts of many of the Exposition buildings, as well as hymns and missionary expository material. Succeeding catalogues were apparently undated; the same electrotype line cuts were used into the twentieth century without change or addition. None shows the spindle-back or bentwood models, possibly because they took too much time to manufacture to make mass production feasible.

The Mt. Lebanon chair industry had been slowly and steadily increasing since 1850, and early in the next decade fell under the management of the vigorous, enterprising and imaginative Bro. Robert Wagan of the Second Family, who advertised widely and built up sales. In 1863 the South Family was officially set off from the Second, and Wagan was appointed First Elder thereof. He proceeded promptly to build a large factory, install modern machinery driven by steam, reorganize the whole enterprise, and standardize and number his products—which came to include not only chairs and footstools, but "shag" cushions and rugs, and oval boxes, sold both singly and in nests of seven (parenthetically, for $3.00!). Fourteen colors were made available in both seating tapes and "shag" cushions and rugs. It is interesting here to note that the Believers bought their woolen worsted tapes in white only, and dyed them at home to fit their needs and orders.

Chair catalogues remained basically unchanged for the succeeding forty years or so; that reproduced in the following pages is taken from a typical undated copy.

For further details on the actual chair industry, the reader is referred to Edward D. and Faith Andrews' *Shaker Furniture,* Appendix A.

Biographical Note:
ELDER ROBERT M. WAGAN
Of the Second, and later of the South Family,
Mt. Lebanon, N.Y. (1833-1883)

Elder Robert established the New Lebanon chair industry on a commercial basis in 1873, although he had had it working up to full production for the preceding ten years. This industry continued long after his death under the same name he had used for it: "R. M. Wagan & Co."—the "Co." being those brethren and sisters who worked in the chair shops. Tens of thousands of chairs and footstools were turned out in the next fifty years, but no other forms of furniture were made for sale to the public. The Shaker chairs generally found in antique shops today came from these Second and South Family factories.

It is a matter of profound regret that no detailed biography of Elder Robert seems to exist. That he was not only a most versatile and imaginative man, but one very highly esteemed, is clear from the memorial to him printed in the *Manifesto* for January 1884, p. 22; even with its rather florid rhetoric, which borders on the sentimental, Elder Robert appears as a most attractive person, richly deserving of the encomium given him. We quote from the most pertinent part of the tribute:

> In early life, a guiding hand from [the] spirit sphere, turned the thoughts, feelings and spiritual aspirations of our departed brother; away from the inharmonies of earth life, away from the strifes and ambitions of a merely worldly existence, to the cause which he so heartily espoused, and for which he so long and faithfully labored. As a child he was tractable and teachable, as a youth he was kind, courteous, loving and obedient; as a man, his noble qualities of head and heart were manifest in all that he said and did. Abroad he always showed himself the true christian gentleman. In business with the children of this world, he was prompt and decided, and honest to the last farthing, yet friendly and affable. At home we had reason to bless him every hour. To the children and youth he was a kind, tender, loving brother, never too tired, or too hurried or worried to say a pleasant word, or present some little token of appreciation, that was helpful and encouraging. To the aged he was particularly deferential and respectful, looking after their interests, anticipating their wants, and ever striving to make them feel that they were a blessing. In temporal things we leaned on him as on a staff that could never fail us. As a leader we were sure he would never lead us astray. As a teacher we had implicit confidence in the truths he taught. As a brother the best beloved. All about us lie tokens of his tender love and care. On every hand are evidences of his ability to scatter blessings in the pathway of those under his charge. Self was ignored, and selfish interests and selfish motives found no place in his noble soul. Each year was a well rounded period in a life well spent.

Surely the portrait of him shown here, taken when he was in his early thirties, gives visible evidence that his eulogist spoke only the truth.

ILLUSTRATED CATALOGUE

AND

PRICE LIST

OF

Shakers' Chairs

MANUFACTURED BY THE

SOCIETY OF SHAKERS.

R. M. WAGAN & CO.,

MOUNT LEBANON, N. Y.

DIRECTIONS

FOR

ORDERING CHAIRS.

As frequent delays and disappointments ensue from a neglect to send definite orders, we are lead to request that you will state the number of chairs wanted, as per illustration.

State definitely the Arms and Rockers. Do you wish both, either, or neither. We do not make the number four with arms; but all other numbers with or without arms and rockers, or with neither arms nor rockers.

State the color of material to be used in seat and back, using number or letter.

The bars across the top of back posts are intended for cushions, but will be furnished to order without additional cost.

State the color of frame wished, as Mahogany, Ebony, or White finish—that is the natural color of the maple wood, for either style the price is the same.

Please send, when you can, shipping orders as to route, railroad, boat, etc., or as freight or express.

Attention to these points will oblige.

INTRODUCTION.

———

WE INVITE the attention of our customers and the public to the contents of this little pamphlet which will give them, in a " concise form," a description and a representation of the different sizes of chairs and foot benches which we manufacture and sell. We would also call the attention of the public to the fact that there is no other chair manufactory which is owned and operated by the Shakers, except the one which is now in operation and owned and operated by the Society of Shakers at Mount Lebanon, Columbia County, N. Y. We deem it a duty we owe the public to enlighten them in this matter, owing to the fact that there are now several manufacturers of chairs who have made and introduced into market an imitation of our styles of chairs, which they sell for Shakers' Chairs, and which are unquestionably bought by the public generally under the impression that they are the real genuine article, made by the Shakers at their establishment in Mount Lebanon. N. Y. Of all the imitations of our chairs which have come under our observation, there are none which we would be willing to accept as our workmanship, nor would we be willing to stake our reputation on their merits.

The increasing demand for our chairs has prompted

us to increase, also, the facilities for producing and improving them. We have spared no expense or labor in our endeavors to produce an article that cannot be surpassed in any respect, and which combines all the advantages of durability, simplicity and lightness.

Since the establishment of our new factory we have been using a very expensive and durable material in the seating of our chairs, with a great variety of colors.

Many of our friends who see the Shakers' chairs for the first time may be led to suppose that the chair business is a new thing for the Shakers to engage in. This is not the fact, however, and may surprise even some of the oldest manufacturers to learn that the Shakers were pioneers in the business after the establishment of the independence of the country.

The heavy wool plush with which we cushion our chairs is a material peculiarly our own. It is made of the best stock and woven in hand looms, and forms a heavy and durable article much more so than anything we are acquainted with. We have all the most desirable and pretty colors represented in our cushions, and they can be all one color, or have a different color border, or with different colored stripes running across the cushion.

We cushion the foot benches to match the cushioned chairs. They are twelve inches square on top with an incline to favor one's feet while sitting in the chair, and they are nicely adapted for the purpose of kneeling stools.

When any of our friends wish any of our chairs they can order them of us by mail, addressed to **R. M. WAGAN & Co., Mt. Lebanon, N. Y.** Our chairs are all nicely wrapped in paper before shipping. It is advisable to ship the chairs by express when there are only a few of them. The expense will be more, but the risk will be less than by freight. We do not ship any goods at our own risk, but deliver them at the nearest or most accessible place of shipping, and there take a receipt for them, showing that they were received in good order, when our obligation ends.

Look for our trade-mark before purchasing—no chair is genuine without it. Our trade-mark is a gold transfer, and is designed to be ornamental.

6

The Shakers' Slat Back Chairs, with Arms and Rockers.

WORSTED LACE SEATS.

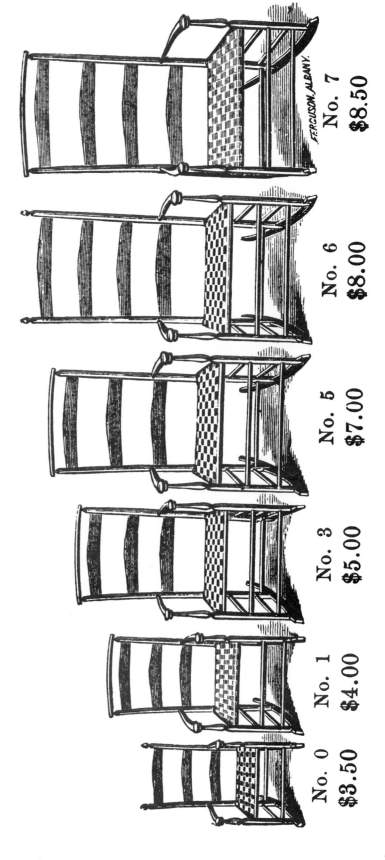

No. 0
$3.50

No. 1
$4.00

No. 3
$5.00

No. 5
$7.00

No. 6
$8.00

No. 7
$8.50

FERGUSON, ALBANY.

The Shakers' Slat Back Chairs, with Rockers.

WORSTED LACE SEATS.

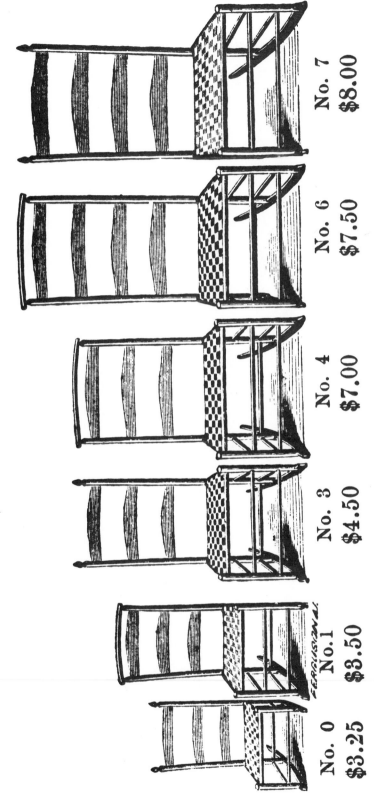

No. 7 $8.00

No. 6 $7.50

No. 4 $7.00

No. 3 $4.50

No. 1 $3.50

No. 0 $3.25

The Shakers' Web Back Chairs, with Arms and Rockers.

WORSTED WEB SEATS AND BACKS.

FERGUSON

No. 0   No. 1   No. 3   No. 5   No. 6   No. 7
$5.00 $5.50 $6.50 $9.50 $10.50 $11.00

The Shakers' Web Back Chairs, with Rockers.

WORSTED WEB SEATS AND BACKS.

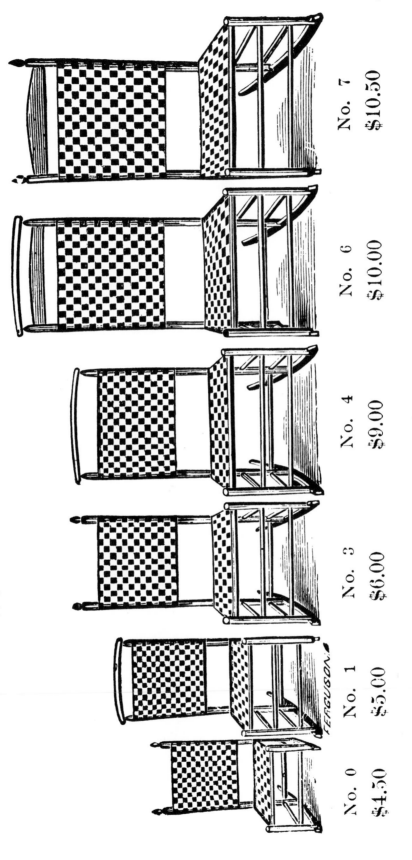

No. 0	No. 1	No. 3	No. 4	No. 6	No. 7
$4.50	$5.00	$6.00	$9.00	$10.00	$10.50

THE SHAKERS' UPHOLSTERED CHAIRS

WITH ARMS AND ROCKERS.

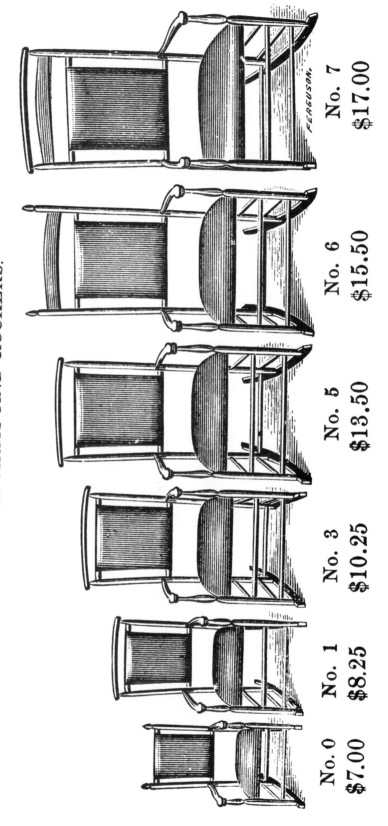

No. 0   No. 1   No. 3   No. 5   No. 6   No. 7
$7.00 $8.25 $10.25 $13.50 $15.50 $17.00

THE SHAKER'S UPHOLSTERED CHAIRS.

WITHOUT ARMS.

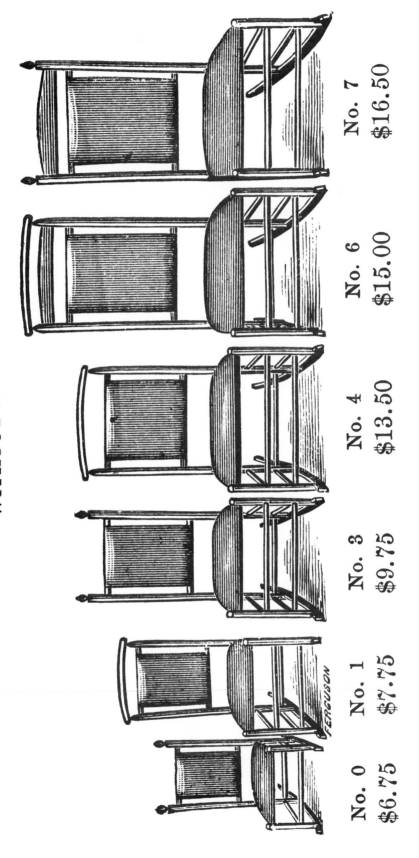

No. 7
$16.50

No. 6
$15.00

No. 4
$13.50

No. 3
$9.75

No. 1
$7.75

No. 0
$6.75

No. 7.   No. 3.

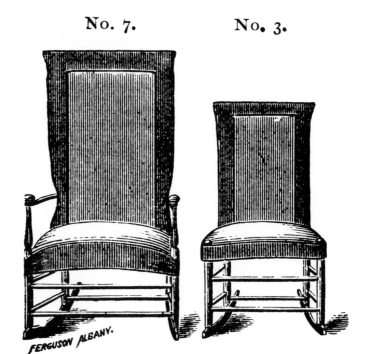

FERGUSON ALBANY.

Price $17.00.   Price $9.75.

Price List of Shakers' Chair Cushions.

Back Cushions.   **Seat Cushions.**

No. 7, each	. . .	$4 00	No. 7, each	. . .	$4 50
6, "	. . .	3 50	6, "	. . .	4 00
5, "	. . .	3 00	5, "	. . .	3 50
4, "	. . .	3 00	4, "	. . .	3 50
3, "	. . .	2 37	3, "	. . .	2 88
1, "	. . .	2 00	1, "	. . .	2 25
0, "	. . .	1 75	0, "	. . .	1 75

Back and Seat Cushions.

No. 7, per set	. .	$8 50	No. 3, per set	. .	$5 25
6, "	. .	7 50	1, "	. .	4 25
5, "	. .	6 50	0, "	. .	3 50
4, "	. .	6 50			

We cushion this Foot Bench to match the Cushioned Chairs, in which manner the most of them are sold.

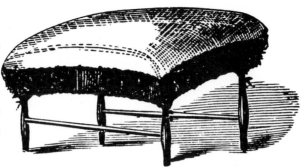

PRICE LIST OF SHAKERS' FOOT BENCHES.

Foot Benches, $1.00; Cushioned, $2.75.
Two-step Benches, $1.50; Cushioned, $3.25.

FLOOR RUGS.

Our Floor Rugs are made of the same material and colors as the cushions. When ordering the Floor Rugs be particular to state the dimensions in length and width; also describe the color of the center and border, if any border is desirable. Our Plush Floor Rugs are sold at the rate of seventy-five cents per square foot.

We also make Wool Rugs and Foot Cushions in the following colors : White, Yellow, Maroon, Blue, Black and Old Gold. Our foot stools are also covered with the above colors of Wool, at same price as with Plush.

☞We were awarded a Diploma and Medal at the Centennial Exhibition for combining in our chairs, Strength, Sprightliness and Modest Beauty.

Price List of Shakers' Chairs
Worsted Lace Seats.
NO ARMS.   NO ROCKERS.

No. 7,	-	-	-	-	-	-	$7 50
6,	-	-	-	-	-	-	7 00
4,	-	-	-	-	-	-	6 50
8,	-	-	-	-	-	-	4 00
1,	-	-	-	-	-	-	3 25
0,	-	-	-	-	-	-	3 00

Price List of Shakers' Chairs
Worsted Lace Seats and Backs.
NO ARMS.   NO ROCKERS.

No. 7,	-	-	-	-	-	-	$10 00
6,	-	-	-	-	-	-	9 50
4,	-	-	-	-	-	-	8 50
3,	-	-	-	-	-	-	5 50
1,	-	-	-	-	-	-	4 50
0,	-	.	-	-	-	-	4 25

Price Chair Frames.

No 7,	-	-	-	-	-	-	$4 50
6,	-	-	-	-	-	.	4 00
5,	-	-	-	-	-	-	3 50
4,	-	-	-	-	-	-	3 00
3,	-	-	-	-	-	-	2 50
1,	-	-	-	-	-	-	2 00
0,	-	-	-	-	-	-	1 75

Price Rocker Frames

No. 7,	-	-	-	-	-	-	$4 75
6,	-	-	-	-	-	-	4 25
5,	-	-	-	-	-	-	3 75
4;	-	-	-	-	-	-	3 25
3,	-	-	-	-	-	-	2 75
1,	-	-	-	-	-	-	2 25
0,	-	-	-	-	-	-	2 00

Price Arm Frames.

No. 7,	-	-	,	-	-	-	$4 75
6,	-	-	-	-	-	-	4 25
5,	-	-	-	-	-	-	3 75
3,	-	-	-	-	-	-	2 75
1,	-	-	-	-	-	-	2 25
0,	-	-	-	-	-	-	2 00

Price Arm Rocker Frames.

No. 7,	-	-	-	-	-	-	$5 00
6,	-	-	-	-	-	-	4 75
5,	-	-	-	-	-	-	4 50
3,	-	-	-	-	-	-	3 50
1,	-	-	-	-	-	-	2 50
0,	-	-	.	-	-	-	2 25

Dimensions of Shakers' Rocking Chair Seats

No. of Chair.	Width.		Depth.		Height of Center. of Seat from Floor
0	12	in.	10	in.	8½ in.
1	14	"	11½	"	12 "
3	18	"	14½	"	
4	21	"	17½	"	
5	19	"	16½	"	14 "
6	21	"	17½	"	
7	22	"	18½	"	

Height of the Back of Chairs.

No.	From Floor.		Above Seat.	
0	23½	in.	16	in.
1	29	"	17½	"
3	35	"	21½	"
4	35	"	22	"
5	38½	"	26	"
6	42½	"	29	"
7	42½	"	29	"

COLORS OF
BRAID AND PLUSH,
Used in our Chairs and Cushions.

Colors of Braid.	Colors of Plush.
No.	Letter.
1 Black.	A Scarlet and Bl'k Stripe.
2 Navy Blue.	B Blue and Black Stripe.
3 Peacock Blue.	C Orange and Bl'k Stripe.
4 Light Blue.	D Blue.
5 Maroon.	E Black.
6 Pomegranate.	F Scarlet.
7 Brown.	G Maroon.
8 Grass Green.	H Orange.
9 Dark Olive.	I Peacock Blue.
10 Light Olive.	J Pomegranate.
11 Old Gold.	K Olive.
12 Drab.	L Old Gold.
13 Scarlet.	M Drab.
14 Orange.	N Ecrue.
Any two of above colors can be used in combination in Seats and Backs, or in solid colors.	Any two of above colors of Plush can be used in combination or solid colors in cushions.

N. B.—Please use numbers and letters when ordering the colors of braid and plush, and mention which you want for center and border of cushions. The plush cannot be used in combination of colors on the *upholstered* chairs : only one color, except the *A, B* and *C*, which are two colors combined in narrow stripe.

SHAKERS'

TRADE MARK.

MT. LEBANON, N. Y.

The above Trade-Mark will be attached to every genuine Shaker Chair, and none others are of our make, notwithstanding any claims to the contrary.

NOTICE.

All persons are hereby cautioned not to use or counterfeit our Trade-Mark.